D1432368

THE ORIGINS OF THE HOLOCAUST:

CHRISTIAN ANTI-SEMITISM

Edited by

RANDOLPH L. BRAHAM

SOCIAL SCIENCE MONOGRAPHS, BOULDER
and
INSTITUTE FOR HOLOCAUST STUDIES OF
THE CITY UNIVERSITY OF NEW YORK
DISTRIBUTED BY COLUMBIA UNIVERSITY PRESS, NEW YORK

1986

EAST EUROPEAN MONOGRAPHS, NO. CCIV

Holocaust Studies Series

Randolph L. Braham, Editor
The Institute for Holocaust Studies
The Graduate School and University Center
The City University of New York

Previously published books in the Series:

Perspectives on the Holocaust, 1982
Contemporary Views on the Holocaust, 1983
Genocide and Retribution, 1983
The Hungarian Jewish Catastrophe.
 A Selected and Annotated
 Bibliography, 1984
Jewish Leadership During the Nazi
 Era: Patterns of Behavior in the
 Free World, 1985
The Holocaust in Hungary. Forty
 Years Later, 1985

The Holocaust Series is published in cooperation with the Institute for Holocaust Studies. These books are outgrowths of lectures, conferences, and research projects sponsored by the Institute. It is the purpose of the series to subject the events and circumstances of the Holocaust to scrutiny by a variety of academics who bring different scholarly disciplines to the study. The first three books in the Series were published by Kluwer-Nijhoff Publishing of Boston.

Printed in the United States of America

CONTENTS

Introduction

This volume is an outgrowth of the fifth major conference organized under the auspices of the Institute for Holocaust Studies of The City University of New York. Held on March 27, 1985, the conference was devoted to the issue of Christian anti-Semitism and its impact on the Holocaust. It was focused on the new, provocative, and controversial theory on the origins of anti-Semitism advanced by Professor Hyam Maccoby of the Leo Baeck College of London. Among the major questions to which Professor Maccoby addressed himself were: "What is it in Christianity that lends itself to anti-Semitism? Is it something accidental, that is not involved in the core of Christian teaching—an unfortunate aberration—or is it something more fundamental? Is Christian anti-Semitism the outcome of a misunderstanding of Christian teaching, or of that teaching itself?"

The linkage between Christian anti-Semitism and the Holocaust has been established in numerous scholarly, theological, and popular works written by Jews and Christians—lay and religious figures alike. Indeed, some of the most candid admissions about the anti-Jewish traditions of Christianity and their responsibility for the Holocaust were made by Christian clergymen. In a report commissioned by the General Synod of the Church of England and published early in 1985, for example, Dr. John Baker, Bishop of Salisbury, stated that Christianity, more than any other religion, succumbed to the disease of racism, and he demonstrated how the poison of anti-Judaism gradually developed into anti-Semitism. In one of the provocative passages of the document, Bishop Baker writes:

> No matter that Jesus was a Jew, that thousands of Jews formed the first Christian churches, that the Jewish scriptures constituted, for nearly 200 years, the only Christian Bible, the Jews were those who had rejected and killed the Son of God; And into that indictment Christians were able to funnel all the hatred and humiliation they themselves felt at having been rejected by Judaism.

Reflecting the opinion voiced by an increasing number of
Christian theologians that the "mere disavowal of anti-
Semitism was not a sufficient response to the Holocaust,"
Bishop Baker stated:

> An act of theological penitence, and a conscious and
> publicly declared reappraisal of the biblical insights,
> including a disowning of the distorted features of
> the New Testament, is essential if the churches are
> to address themselves to their part in the racial situa-
> tion with cleansed consciences.

Bishop Baker's position comes quite close to that represented by Professor Maccoby. However, Professor Maccoby
was more persuasive in demonstrating that anti-Semitism is
much more deeply embedded in the New Testament than
many progressive Christian theologians are ready to admit.
In his view, anti-Semitism "forms an essential ingredient in
the Christian myth of redemption." He summarizes the
three major strands in Christian anti-Semitism as follows:
"The first, derived from Gnosticism, providing the dualism
by which Jews are regarded as the people of the Devil; the
second, derived from Judaism, providing the concept of
the Church as the vehicle of God's promises. . . ; the third,
and most important of all, is derived from the mystery-
cults: the concept of the crucified God who saves the world
from the consequences of its sins, and who needs the dark
figure of the Sacred Executioner [the Jews] to accomplish
his salvific death and to take upon himself the evil but necessary role of murderer, thus assuming the role of acolyte
of Satan, the evil god."

Professor Maccoby had a distinguished panel of discussants to contend with. They responded to the challenge of
his thesis with a formidable display of erudition and critical analysis. The discussants were: Dr. Robert A. Everett,
Pastor of Emanuel United Church of Christ, Irvington, N.J.;
Dr. Eugene J. Fisher, Executive Secretary of the Secretariat
for Catholic-Jewish Relations of the National Conference
of Catholic Bishops, Washington, D.C.; Rabbi A. James

Rudin, National Director of Interreligious Affairs of the American Jewish Committee; and Rabbi Marc H. Tanenbaum, Director of International Relations of the American Jewish Committee.

Dr. Alan T. Davies, Professor of Religious Studies at Victoria College, University of Toronto, could not attend the conference. He summarized his reaction to Professor Maccoby's thesis in a letter dated February 15, 1985 (see page 60).

Through their views and interpretations the participants in the conference have made a valuable contribution not only to a better understanding of the problems that plagued Jewish-Christian relations for almost two millenia, but also to the advancement of the cause of pluralism and toleration. Needless to say, these views and interpretations are theirs alone and do not necessarily reflect those of the editor or of the Institute for Holocaust Studies.

This volume could not have been completed without the cooperation of the contributors, who invested the same energy and erudition in it as they did in the conference. For this I am deeply indebted to them. I would also like to express my appreciation to President Harold M. Proshansky and Dean Solomon Goldstein of the Graduate School and University Center of The City University of New York for their consistent support for Holocaust Studies. Finally, I would like to thank the Holocaust Survivors Memorial Foundation, the primary supporter of the Institute, and the many contributors to the Special Holocaust Research and Publication Fund for their generosity.

Randolph L. Braham
February 1986

The Origins of Anti-Semitism

Hyam Maccoby

Anti-Semitism, if defined as merely an intense dislike of Jews coupled with a tendency to ascribe a wide range of evils to their agency, did not begin with Christianity: one may cite Manetho, Apion and Seneca. Even the more radical anti-Semitism that sees Jews as the earthly agents of a *cosmic* force for evil did not begin with Christianity; we can see this syndrome in Sethian Gnosticism, which, as recent research makes probable, existed before the advent of Christianity. But Christianity is the channel through which this radical anti-Semitism was transmitted to the medieval and modern world. The idea of the Jews as the people of the Devil, predestined for an evil role in history, can be found in the Gospels (e.g., *Matthew 23*, and pervasively in *John*), was fully developed in the writings of the Church Fathers, and was further elaborated in the Middle Ages (see Trachtenberg, *The Devil and the Jews*). Modern anti-Semitism has made full use of this ancient and medieval material.

The question is: What is it in Christianity that lends itself to anti-Semitism? Is it something accidental, not involved in the core of Christian teaching—an unfortunate aberration— or is it something more fundamental? Is Christian anti-Semitism the outcome of a misunderstanding of Christian teaching, or is it essential to the teaching itself?

In recent years the long-cherished solution that anti-Semitism is not to be found in the New Testament, but arose in the Church as a misinterpretation of the New Testament, has proved increasingly hard to sustain. Most serious scholars now admit that it is in the New Testament itself, and the question becomes: How deeply embedded in the New Testament? Is it detachable from the main core of the New Testament's message, or not? Various answers have been given.

The answer associated with Rosemary Ruether is that the anti-Semitism of the New Testament arose from the needs of Christian rivalry with Judaism. In order to cope with the continuing existence of Judaism as an independent religion not acknowledging Jesus as the Messiah, it was found necessary to denigrate Judaism and, consequently, the Jews. The myth was created—and embodied in certain New Testament passages—that the Jews had always been an evil people who had consistently rejected the prophets sent to them by God; the final rejection of Jesus was thus merely the culmination of this pattern. The prophets of the Old Testament were thus not regarded as Jews, nor credited to Judaism; instead they were regarded as proto-Christians, and the archetypal role given to the Jews was that of rejectionists and backsliders.

This analysis offers some hope for the continuance of Christianity as a religion purged of anti-Semitism. For anti-Semitism enters Christianity, on this view, in a nonfundamental way as the outcome of religious rivalry, rather than as the expression of any essential doctrine. The solution, then, lies in the recognition of Judaism as an independent religion; some writers, building on Ruether's analysis (e.g., Gaston and Gager) have argued that the basis of such a recognition of Judaism as a religion of independent validity exists also in the New Testament, in the writings of Paul. All writers of the Ruether school, however, agree that the myth of an evil Jewry exists in the later books of the New Testament, including the Gospels, and that therefore some excision or demotion of New Testament material is necessary to the continuance of Christianity.

I welcome the analysis of the Ruether school as a great advance, and an emancipation from the standpoint—still held by the great majority even of those Christians concerned about Christian anti-Semitism—that the New Testament itself is free of anti-Semitism. I hold, however, that the Ruether analysis does not go nearly far enough. Anti-Semitism is much more deeply embedded in the New Testament than this acknowledges; for anti-Semitism is not merely an extraneous outcome of religious rivalry but forms an essential ingredient in the Christian myth of redemption. The Jews have a role to play among the *dramatis personae* of this myth, and are not merely a religious group to be superseded or discredited. It is through the role assigned to the Jews in this drama, and its profound imaginative impact, that anti-Semitism has been transmitted, and has survived in secular form in post-Christian communities such as Nazi Germany and Soviet Russia.

If the Jewish rejection of Jesus were the key to Christian anti-Semitism, there would be no difference in quality between Christian and Muslim hostility to the Jews, since the Jews also rejected Muhammad. In fact, however, there is a world of difference. Muslim hostility to Jews is on the same level as Muslim hostility to Christians, and though this has often led to violence and persecution, there has been no *diabolization* of the Jews in traditional Islamic thinking. (Though in very recent times, for political motives, diabolization of the Jews has occurred in Islam but, significantly, with material drawn from Christian sources such as the blood-libel and the *Protocols of the Elders of Zion*, since Islamic tradition contains no such materials.)

In Christendom, however, the Jews were diabolized, and this arises not from Jewish rejection of Jesus, but from the Jewish mythic role as the murderers, or deicides, of Jesus. Murder alone would not have produced this diabolization, for the judicial murder of Socrates by the Athenians, for example, had no such outcome; but the alleged judicial murder of Jesus (historically incorrect) by the Jews was combined with the deification of Jesus, so producing the mythic crime of deicide. Even this would not have produced the depth of loathing and metaphysical fear involved in anti-Semitism, were it not that the death of Jesus was mythologized as a *cosmic sacrifice*, so that the Jews figure in the myth as the sacrificers of God. Though they do not intend his death as a sacrifice, but rather act from motives of malice, they bring about a necessary death that functions as salvific for members of the Christian Church.

The Jews thus figure in the central Christian myth of salvation in a role that can be paralleled elsewhere in mythology. A god who brings salvation by his death is often coupled with an evil power or god who brings about the necessary death: thus Osiris is killed by Set, Baal by Mot, Baldur by Loki. The figure of Judas, in the Gospels, has just this quality of fated evil; but Judas is merely the eponymous representative of the Jewish people as a whole, and has been so understood throughout the history of Christian anti-Semitism. Judas betrays Jesus because Satan "enters" him, and Satan is the evil deity who strictly corresponds to Set, Mot or Loki. The Jews are his earthly acolytes, and are regarded as Satanic. The role of Satan as engineer of the death of the divine Sacrifice has no analogy in Judaism, and therefore the Christian Satan is a new creation of Christian mythology, with analogies only in pagan sacrificial myths.

Mythology has its roots in anthropology, and we may ask: What was the ritual in which myths of the slaying of a good god by an evil god were grounded? The answer is to be found in rituals of human sacrifice. Where a human sacrifice is performed at times of great stress (especially at the foundation or threatened destruction of a city or a tribe), the guilt of the deed of blood was often shifted to the figure of an Executioner, who was cursed and driven into the desert, but who retained some sanctity as the performer of the deed that saved the tribe. The story of Cain is the remnant of such a ritual, but with its abhorrence of human sacrifice the Hebrew Bible has changed the sacrifice of Abel into plain murder; yet the immunity of Cain, however, preserves a feature of the original story. When the Church Fathers identified the Jews with Cain and Jesus with Abel, they sensed the sacrificial overtones of the Cain and Abel story.

The Jews perform the role of Sacred Executioner for Christian society, and this accounts for the strange mixture of loathing and awe that characterizes anti-Semitism. When the Executioner of the divine sacrifice is cursed and driven into the desert, the tribe washes its hands—like Pilate—of the responsibility for the murderous deed that has brought their salvation. Since the tribe depends utterly on the death of the victim for its salvation, it *wants* him to die. But this desire inspires great guilt, which is projected as hatred onto the person deputed to perform the sacrifice. The more the executioner is hated and cursed, the more the tribe feels absolved for the murder which, in reality, they have themselves arranged.

The remedy to anti-Semitism does not lie in cosmetic excisions of "rejectionist" passages in the New Testament, nor in exhortations to recognize Judaism as an independent religion, much as these measures are to be welcomed. It lies in radical criticism of the central Christian myth of salvation, as a means of shifting guilt and responsibility: the main burden of guilt is transferred to Jesus himself, but the secondary guilt involved in sacrifice itself is shifted to the Jews. Areas to be tackled are: the deification of Jesus; the concept of atonement; the Jews as embodiments of the worst in human nature, or as representatives of Satan. Post-Christian secular versions of anti-Semitism should be analyzed through their relationship to the Christian myth, and treated as "rationalizations," by which the main elements of that myth are given a would-be scientific rationale.

So far in this paper I have given a rapid survey of my view of anti-Semitism as a phenomenon rooted in a religious myth. In the rest of this paper, I will go into certain aspects of the matter in more detail in order to give a more rounded picture of my thesis and of its possibilities as a program for research and education. My full view is that there are three main elements in Christian anti-Semitism: one derived from Gnosticism, one from Judaism, and one from mystery-religion.

I mentioned that Christianity was not alone in the ancient world in describing the Jews as the agents of a cosmic force for evil, but that this had already been done in certain Gnostic sects. Is there, then, a historical connection between Gnostic anti-Semitism and that of Christianity? I believe that there is, and I am engaged on a program of research at present, for the

Hebrew University of Jerusalem, to establish this connection. Gnostic anti-Semitism may be seen, for example, in the pre-Christian Sethian document *The Apocalypse of Adam*. The characteristic myth of Gnostic anti-Semitism is that the world was created by an evil God, the Demiurge, who in giving the Torah to the Jews, made them his chosen people. Nevertheless, the true High God has transmitted the true *gnosis* through a line of initiates beginning with Seth. Characteristically, Gnostic anti-Semitism selects from the Hebrew Bible non-Jewish personalities, such as Seth, Enoch, Melchizedek, as the guardians and transmitters of a tradition of knowledge, or *gnosis*, which rivals and surpasses the Torah, and relegates the Jews to an inferior position as the acolytes of a false God. Because of its Jewish content, drawn from the Hebrew Bible, Gnosticism has sometimes been described as Jewish in origin. A better understanding of the matter, in my view, is that Gnostic anti-Semitism arose among Hellenistic non-Jewish groups who were fascinated by the Hebrew Bible and the claims of the Jews to chosenness, but who reacted by turning the Jewish material on its head, and so producing an anti-Semitic myth. It is a case of cultural rivalry and envy; an ambivalent love-hate relationship to Judaism led to a myth expressing the desire to supplant and usurp the Jewish position as favorites of God, but coopted Jewish literature to create such a myth. Once fashioned, the myth acts as a vehicle for aggressive feelings toward the Jews and as a powerful agent of anti-Semitic propaganda, which without the myth's broad imaginative appeal would remain on an abstract level.

The Christian anti-Semitic myth is partly adapted from the Gnostic anti-Semitic myth. The Torah is not described as evil, but as limited. It was not given by an evil God, but by limited supernatural beings, angels, to show that it was intended to have a limited validity. The world was not created by an evil God, but it has fallen under the rule of one, Satan ("the Prince of this world"), and the Jews, by continuing to revere the Torah after its validity had ceased, have become the minions of Satan. Thus Christianity presents a moderate form of the dualism of the Gnostic myth, somewhat watered down, but still retaining the anti-Semitic picture of the Jews based on Biblical materials.

On the other hand, another aspect of the Gnostic myth is *not* watered down in Christianity, but accentuated. This is the supersessionary, or "replacement" element. Gnosticism provided a rival or alternative tradition to that of Judaism; instead of the Jewish succession of prophets, an alternative was posited, a succession of lone voices, bearers of *gnosis* pointing to an other-worldly solution to the ills of this world. Christianity, on the other hand (and this is Rosemary Ruether's main contribution to the study of Christian anti-Semitism), carried out a much larger-scale usurpation. It took over the Jewish prophets themselves, as Christians or proto-Christians. It also took over the whole historical sweep of Judaism—its plan of world-history from the creation of Adam to the Last Days—thus giving Christianity a kind of universalism lacking in Gnosticism, which had a historical succession of lone figures, but no sense of the historical mission of a community. Islam later carried out a similar usurpation of both Judaism and Christianity: Abraham was represented as a Muslim, and the story of the Akedah was re-worked with Ishmael—ancestor of the Arabs—instead of Isaac as the central figure. This element of usurpation is thus a powerful source of anti-Semitism, as Ruether argues: but, in itself, is no greater than the similar process in Islam which produced Muslim anti-Semitism and anti-Christianism. This I would describe as the second element in Christian anti-Semitism—the element derived from Judaism itself, the incorporation of the Jewish historical scheme, necessitating the ousting of the Jews themselves from this schema.

Also, it should be pointed out that the Gnostic supersessionary method of the *alternative* tradition is not entirely lacking in Christianity, in the use of Biblical non-Jewish personalities, such as Melchizedek and Enoch, to demonstrate the existence of a non-Jewish *gnosis* superior to the Torah.

The third and deepest element in Christianity, with which I am myself concerned in *The Sacred Executioner*, is that derived from the mystery-cults. This element introduces into Christianity a type of anti-Semitism that is more virulent than that of the Gnostic cults. In the Gnostic myth, a succession of redeemer-figures is pictured as descending into the world and sometimes suffering persecution at the hands of the Jews; but this is not a central feature, and the main aim of the redeemer is to impart *gnosis*, not to suffer a sacrificial death. Christianity, however, has given a central position to the element of violence. The redeemer figure of Gnosticism has been amalgamated with the redeemer figure of the mystery-cults, in which a dying-and-resurrected god brings immortality to his worshippers by his sacrificial death. The mystery-cults themselves were *not* anti-Semitic, since the figure of the Sacred Executioner in them was that of a rival god, and no human group was identified as his acolyte. The anti-Semitism of the Gnostic sects identified the Jews, a recognizable human group, as the enemies of *gnosis*, but it was left to Christianity to deepen the guilt of the Jews by turning the redeemer into a unique sacrificial figure rather than one of a succession of bringers of *gnosis*. The uniqueness of Christianity lies precisely in this amalgamation of Gnosticism with mystery-religion to form an anti-Semitic myth of unprecedented potency. The mystery-cults were local in their reference. Gnosticism, on the other hand, was a universal belief, providing a way of salvation for all mankind, and speaking to the human condition itself. This universality (of a cosmic, not historical, type), gave the Jews an evil universality, as representatives of cosmic evil and enemies of the universal solution to the human problem. This universality was taken into Christian anti-Semitism, with the extra dimension given by the concept of a unique redeemer who saved mankind not through *gnosis* but by his sacrificial death brought about by the powers of evil through the instrumentality of the Jews.

By what steps, then, was the Christian anti-Semitic myth established? Jesus himself, and his earliest followers in the Jerusalem Church (so-called, for it was not really a church), had no notion of any anti-Semitic myth, for they were practicing Jews themselves, and were looking forward to a messianic age, or kingdom of God, in which the Jews would be the honored priest-nation of the world, not cosmic villains. Jesus, in my view, never thought of himself as a divine figure, but as the promised king-messiah who would restore Jewish independence and inaugurate an era of world peace, as prophesied by Isaiah and Zechariah. His enemies, therefore, were not the Jews but the Romans, whose military empire stood in the way of the messianic era of world peace. His death was not regarded either by him or his Jewish followers as a divine sacrifice to atone for the sins of mankind.

It was Paul who created the Christian myth by deifying Jesus for the first time, and by regarding his death as a cosmic sacrifice in which the powers of evil sought to overwhelm the power of good, but, against their will, only succeeded in bringing about a salvific event. We find already in the writings of Paul the concept of the Jews as the unwitting agents of salvation, whose malice in bringing about the death of Jesus is turned to good because this is the very thing needed for the salvation of sinful mankind. The combination of malice and blindness described here is the exact analogue of the myth of Baldur, in Norse mythology, in which malice is personified by the wicked god Loki and blindness by the blind god Hother, and both together bring about the salvific death, which alone guarantees a good crop and salvation from death by famine. Thus Paul is the creator of the Christian myth, in that he, by an imaginative stroke, combined the salvation aspect of the mystery-religions with the universality and dualism of the Gnostic cults, so incidentally creating cosmic villains, the Jews, too, while retaining the historical salvation-scheme of Judaism. This whole conception arises from Paul's de-politicization of the historical Jesus, by which he was divested of all political attributes as a Jew of his period, and turned into an a-historical figure, a visitant from outer space with a purely spiritual mission devoid of political content. This was called a "stroke of genius" by Bousset in that it diverted Christianity from conflict with Rome, which was no longer the enemy, being merely a political entity. Instead, on the spiritual plane, the Jews became the enemy; though this anti-

political stance was itself an astute political move, since it
substituted a defeated, weak political entity, the Jews, as
the archetypal enemy, for a powerful political entity,
Rome. The way was thus prepared for an accommodation
between Pauline Christianity and Rome, and even for the
adoption by Rome of Christianity as its official faith, with
its center at Rome itself—an outcome which the loyal Jew,
Jesus, with his veneration of Jerusalem as the spiritual center
of the world, would have found astonishing and dismaying.

The myth adumbrated by Paul was then brought into
full imaginative life in the Gospels, which were all written
under the influence of Paul's ideas and for the use of the
Pauline Christian Church. A full-rounded narrative of mythological dimensions is now elaborated on the basis of historical materials, which are adapted to provide a melodrama
of good and evil. The powerful image of Judas Iscariot is
created: a person fated and even designated by his victim,
Jesus, to perform the evil deed, possessed by Satan and
carrying out his evil role by compulsion, yet suffering the
fate of the accursed—a perfect embodiment of the role of
the Sacred Executioner, deputed to perform the deed of
blood, yet execrated for performing it. While Judas per-
forms the role on the personal level, the Jewish people per-
forms it on the communal level: actuated by blindness and
malice in alternation, calling for Jesus' crucifixion in the
climactic Barabbas scene and accepting responsibility for
the sacrifice by saying, "His blood be on us and on our
children!" (*Mt* 27:25) What in Paul's letters was just the
outline of a myth has become definite and replete with
narrative quality, an instrument for cultural indoctrination
and the conveyor of indelible impressions to children who
are told the tale. At the same time, the responsibility is
carefully removed from the Romans: their cruel, rapacious
rule of Judea is softened into a benevolent paternalism, their
chief representative, Pontius Pilate, (who was actually a
bloodthirsty moneygrubber) is represented as well-meaning
and mild. All political aspects of Jesus are obliterated (being shunted into the invented person of his *doppleganger*

Jesus Barabbas), and thus the sole responsibility for his death is laid at the door of the Jewish leaders. To this end, fictitious religious conflict between Jesus and the Pharisees is introduced, and his conflict with the High Priest, which was actually political, is represented as religious. Jesus, by being made into an atoning sacrifice in a cosmic war between good and evil, has been removed from all political realities and from the actual circumstances of his death. The whole story, by being removed to the mythological level, has mythologized the Jews too.

In the subsequent history of the Church, the mythological role of the Jews as deicides and sacrificers of the incarnate God is elaborated and the Jews are further demonized. This process took several centuries to accomplish fully, for ordinary Christians tended at first to treat Jews as ordinary human beings with whom they could have normal social relations. Several councils of the Church forbade such social relations, and great Christian preachers such as St. John Chrysostom denounced all friendliness towards the Jews and built up the picture of the Jews as an accursed nation with whom no Christian should fraternize. Yet the Jews as they were placed more and more in the role of a pariah class in Christendom (by being forbidden to take part in all normal vocations) fulfilled a societal role, just as they filled a necessary role in Christian mythology. Their role was similar to that played in Hindu society by the Untouchables, except that the latter do the physical dirty work of society, while the Jews, in the Christian economy, do the moral dirty work, which is regarded as necessary, but unfit for Christians; it is therefore fortunate that there is a class of damned persons which is available to perform this work. Thus the Jews were pushed into the activity of "usury," forbidden by the Church, but actually essential to the economy. In many areas, the Jews were forced to provide the public executioner of criminals; who better than the Jews, the performers of the necessary murder or execution of Jesus, to perform the official bloodshed of Christian society?

The performance of a necessary function, however hated and despised, was a kind of protection to the Jews. By being always present as the suffering culprits, paying endlessly for their murder of Jesus, they lifted the guilt of that murder from Christians, who by venting their moral indignation on the Jews could feel themselves to be accepted by Christ. Moreover, a saying of Paul gave rise to the belief that the Second Coming of Christ could only occur when the Jews became converted to Christianity; this belief saved the Jews from annihilation on many occasions. At the time of the Second Coming, however, it was believed that the Jews would disappear, either by being absorbed into the Church as converts, or (a more sinister alternative) by being annihilated in the wars of the Antichrist against Christ at the time of his Second Coming. The latter alternative was held by millenarian sects, and had respectable backing in Christian literature, but was on the whole frowned on by the official Church, as it led to populist outbreaks that could turn against the Church itself and its temporal leaders.

At the time of the Second Coming, the Jews would no longer be necessary, because the sacrifice of Jesus would no longer be necessary. Christ Triumphant appears when the problem of human sin (which gave rise to the need for a divine sacrifice in the first place) has been finally conquered. When a suffering Jesus on the cross is no longer needed, a demonic people acting as his accursed executioners is also no longer needed; they can disappear, either by conversion or by annihilation. At times of millenarian excitement, the method of annihilation was indeed tried; this was the aim of the mobs who carried out huge massacres of Jews at the time of the Crusades. Millenarian movements often contained the scenario that the Antichrist would be a Jew who would be hailed by the Jews as their Messiah, and would actually set up a Jewish Empire based on a rebuilt Temple in Jerusalem, but would be defeated by the armies of Christ, when the Jews would be annihilated to the last man. This scenario lies behind the secular, post-Christian millenarian movement of Hitler, in which Hitler himself took the role of Christ Triumphant, and in which many of the slogans of Christian millenarianism—including the "Thousand Year Reich" —were employed.

Post-Christian anti-Semitism can thus be more dangerous to the Jews than Christian anti-Semitism itself, for in post-Christian anti-Semitism, the moral restraints of Christianity have disappeared, and the naked myth of the demonized Jews remains, in an atmosphere of populist millenarianism where the possibility of a pure, *Judenrein* Utopia is envisaged. In the Christian Churches themselves, a new spirit of awareness of Christian responsibility for anti-Semitism already exists, though it has not yet sufficiently reached the lower levels of teaching; nor is the harm done by the simple outlines of the Christian myth sufficiently realized, but on the contrary, it is thought that the beauty of the Christian myth as an edifying story has survived the onslaughts of modern Biblical research. It is only when the phenomenology of the myth itself—quite apart from the question of its historical inaccuracy—is subjected to searching criticism that real progress will be made in combating anti-Semitism, and that this endeavor will be of benefit not only to Christians, but also to post-Christians of every kind, whether of the Left or of the Right, or of middle-of-the-road liberal agnosticism, all of whom are more affected than they think by the Christian myth as it relates to the Jews, whom they have not yet succeeded as seeing as normal human beings, rather than as actors in a nightmare mythological drama.

To sum up, then, I would argue that there are three strands in Christian anti-Semitism: the first, derived from Gnosticism, provides the dualism by which the Jews are regarded as the people of the Devil; the second, derived from Judaism, provides the concept of the Church as the vehicle of God's promises moving through history from the Creation to the Last Days, and this brings Christianity into collision with the community of Israel from whom these claims are usurped; the third, and most important of all, is derived from the mystery-cults: the concept of the crucified God who saves the world from the consequences of its sins, and who needs the dark figure of the Sacred Executioner to accomplish his salvific death and to take upon himself the evil but necessary role of murderer, thus assuming the role of acolyte of Satan, the evil god. Out of this came the cry, "Who killed Christ?" This is the cry that was heard at the time of Hitler's Holocaust and at every other massacre of Jews in Christendom: this is the reason that Hitler's massacre of the Jews met with silent acquiescence from the vast majority of his subjects. Though public outcry and protests from the Pope brought a quick end to Hitler's program for the extermination of the insane and unfit, no such outcry or protest was forthcoming about the Jews. For it is endemic in Christendom that the Jews, the murderers of God, deserve all possible sufferings.

BIBLIOGRAPHY

Wilhelm Bousset, "Antichrist." In: *Encyclopaedia of Religion and Ethics*, John Hastings, ed., Edinburgh: T. & T. Clark, 1908, vol.1, pp. 578-581.

Alan T. Davies, ed., *Antisemitism and the Foundations of Christianity*. New York: Paulist Press, 1979.

John C. Gager, *The Origins of Anti-Semitism*. New York, Oxford University Press, 1983.

John Hick, ed., *The Myth of God Incarnate*. London: SCM, 1978.

Hyam Maccoby, "Jesus and Barabbas." *New Testament Studies*, Cambridge, vol. xvi, 1968, pp. 55-60.

Hyam Maccoby, *Revolution in Judaea*. New York: Taplinger, 1980.

Hyam Maccoby, *The Sacred Executioner*. London/New York: Thames & Hudson, 1982, pp. 97-186.

Hyam Maccoby, *Judaism on Trial: Jewish-Christian Disputations in the Middle Ages*. East Brunswick: Associated University Presses, 1982, pp. 19-94.

Rosemary Ruether, *Faith and Fratricide*. New York: Seabury Press, 1974.

Herman L. Strack, *Das Blut im Glauben und Aberglauben*, 8th ed. Leipzig: J. C. Hinrichs, 1911. (Schriften des Institutum Judaicum in Berlin, Nr. 14.)
English version: *The Jew and Human Sacrifice*. Translated by H. Blanchamp. London: Cope and Fenwick, 1909.

G. Stroumsa, *Another Seed: Studies in Sethian Gnosticism*. Leiden: E. J. Brill, 1984.

Joshua Trachtenberg, *The Devil and the Jews*. New York: Harper & Row, 1966.

RESPONSES

The Origins of Anti-Semitism in Christian Theology:
A Reaction and Critique

Eugene J. Fisher

In the works of Hyam Maccoby on this subject which I
have seen to date,[1] two major themes seem to predominate:
first, that (in the words of his original outline for this conference) "anti-Semitism, in its medieval and modern forms,
can be traced to the picture of the Jews given in the New
Testament;" and second, that anti-Semitism is not peripheral
to central Christian doctrines such as salvation, redemption,
atonement, etc., but constitutive of them on the level of
myth so that, if dialogue is to proceed between Jews and
Christians the latter must abandon or at least radically alter
their core beliefs. Along the latter line of reasoning, Professor Maccoby charges Christianity with being, among other
things, essentially gnostic and dualistic, non-monotheistic
and with holding a pessimistic world view, as compared
with the benign realism and relative anthropological opti-
mism of Judaism.

Maccoby acknowledges, in the original conference outline, that the first theme is not a new one. Indeed it is not.
Since first articulated (though with much more nuancing
and historical sensitivity) by Jules Isaac in the late 1940s
and early 1950s, a large and significant body of scholarly
literature has developed.[2] The second theme, while presenting some interesting new wrinkles, is also not entirely new.
Major elements (the charges of gnosticism, otherworldli-
ness, theological pessimism, Paul as perverter of Jesus'
teaching, etc.) find their own origins in the apologetics of
the *Wissenschaft des Judentums* movement of nineteenth
century Germany and even in Jewish medieval polemical
literature.[3]

Anti-Judaism and Anti-Semitism

That there is a relationship, both historical and concep-
tual, between the Christian "teaching of contempt" against
Jews and Judaism, on the one hand, and modern forms of
anti-Semitism on the other, neither can nor need be denied.
The proper Christian approach today, as outlined by the
Second Vatican Council and in more detail in subsequent
official Church teaching,[4] is that the "teaching of contempt" must be systematically dismantled since it rested
on false premises, historically and theologically. Thus, the
Council specifically condemned the deicide charge[5] and
imposed a normative hermeneutic for subsequent Catholic
interpretation of the New Testament text: ". . . the Jews
should not be represented as rejected by God or accursed,
as if this followed from Holy Scripture."[6]

The theological line of interpretation of the New Testament which resulted in the medieval teaching of contempt
and prepared the ground, as it were, for the emergence of
modern anti-Semitism is thus officially precluded today.
The move in this direction has rightly been described by
Professor Tommaso Federici of Rome as "irreversible."[7]
The "irreversibility" of *Nostra Aetate*, of course, is an aspect that Maccoby's second thesis would call into question,
since if he is correct that anti-Semitism is essential to
Church doctrine, the Council's resounding "no" to it cannot be more than a passing fancy. The recent statement by
Pope John Paul II to the American Jewish Committee delegation in Rome, however, would seem to bolster Federici's
rather than Maccoby's interpretation of the official status
of the Conciliar declaration. There, twenty years after
Nostra Aetate promulgation, the Pope described the document as an "expression of the Faith" and "word of the
Divine Wisdom."[8]

Maccoby's approach to the relationship between the
acknowledged anti-Judaic polemics embedded in various
New Testament traditions and the specific phenomenon of
modern anti-Semitism revealed to us in all its horror at
Auschwitz can perhaps best be described as the "straight

line method" of historical accounting. He admits virtually no distinction between Nazism's racial attitudes towards Jews and the attitudes of Paul and the other New Testament authors, despite the fact that the latter were—and felt they remained—Jews.

Such a leap over the chasm of two millenia of historical change and development is a long one. And Maccoby, in my view, falls somewhat short of proving his case, especially as he tends to presume the conclusion rather than developing argumentation to support it. As indicated above, there is now a substantial body of literature on the subject,[9] and an emerging scholarly consensus. Alan T. Davies, summarizing the views of a dozen leading thinkers in the field who contributed essays to his volume in reaction to what Maccoby calls "the Reuther School," states:

> If a common motif in these essays can be described, it is the conviction that Christians need not choose between an ideological defense of their scriptures that wards off damaging criticism and the sad conclusion that the New Testament is so wholly contaminated by anti-Jewish prejudice as to lose all moral authority Instead, through careful study, Christians can isolate what genuine forms of anti-Judaism really color the major writings, and, by examining their historic genesis, neutralize their potential for harm.[10]

Maccoby's straight line method fails the critical test of providing an explanation that can account for the vast number of historical realities and ambiguities presented by the record. It simply does not account for the positive side of the ambivalent New Testament and Patristic attitudes toward Jews and Judaism which, for example, John Townsend finds in John and Lloyd Gaston in Paul in their essays for the Davies volume. Nor does it account for actual Christian behavior toward Jews over the centuries.

Distinctions need to be made in the various periods. As Samuel Sandmel, of blessed memory, pointed out in *Anti-Semitism in the New Testament?* "the nineteenth—and twentieth-century word *anti-Semitism* is a completely

wrong term when transferred to the first and second Chris-
tian centuries."[11] Specifically Christian hostility toward
Jews and Judaism was religious in character, Nazi anti-
Semitism was racist and nationalist.[12]

Sandmel goes on to point out, chapter by chapter, anti-
Judaic and anti-Jewish elements in the New Testament.
Certainly there are polemics against, for example, rabbinic
Judaism in Matthew, for example in *Mt.* 23 (*Mt.* 23 is not,
contrary to Maccoby, anti-Jewish as such, but, rather, limits
its attack to "scribes and Pharisees," from whose ranks
came the later rabbis who are Matthew's real target.) One
must not overconclude from a single instance of the term
"devil," as Maccoby does in citing *Mt.* 23:15 as a "diabolization" of "the Jews." Peter, surely not a symbol of Jews,
is called "Satan" twice. (*Mt.* 16:23; *Mk* 8:33). Judas, by
the way, is called "a devil" only once, in John (*Jn* 6:70:
"yet *one of you* is a devil;" but cf. *Jn.* 13:2: "The devil
had already put it in the mind of Judas").

Recent works have set into much sharper relief than
even a few years ago the necessity for distinguishing between theological polemic and modern racial anti-Semitism.
St. Paul's writings can be called polemical, but hardly racist (e.g., *Romans* 9-11). Indeed, while it might have been
seen to be reasonable to accept Maccoby's "straight line
method" fifteen or twenty years ago, the scholarship of
the intervening period has shown such oversimplification
to be untenable. John G. Gager, cited by Maccoby,[13] and
Robert L. Wilken[14] each effectively demolish as anachron-
istic such attempts as Maccoby's to read literature written
in the fourth century or earlier as if it had been set down
by Wilhelm Marr in the nineteenth.

This, of course, is not to deny the historical links between the ancient interreligious polemics and the tenor of
society that could produce a Hitler and have his views so
widely acceptable. But to equate the two is to establish, in
a chronological framework, a "collective guilt" charge in
its own way as problematical—and certainly as spurious—as
that one wishes to defeat.

Maccoby cites also Joshua Trachtenberg's classic, *The Devil and the Jews: The Medieval Conception of the Jew and Its Relation to Modern Anti-Semitism* (Jewish Publication Society, 1943).[15] Here, in one sense, he is on safer ground. For it is precisely in this period (and I would argue not effectively before this period) that the demonization of the Jews appears to have occurred. Dating from this period, and only from this period, are the key canards and stereotypes (blood libel, Jews portrayed as devils, etc.) that functioned to bolster the Nazi anti-Semitic propaganda machine. Only with this period does the invidious *Judensau* begin to appear on churches, such as the Cathedral at Regensburg.

Indeed, in a recent major work Jeremy Cohen has argued, I believe definitively, that this period saw a major *qualitative* change in Christian theological attitudes and actual practices toward Jews and Judaism. Before this time, one does not find a full demonization of the Jews, nor do they play much of a key role in the central "Christian myth" or "cosmic drama" to which Maccoby refers. Significantly, it is only with this period that the *Talmud* suffers widespread attacks.[16] None of the central creeds of the early Councils, the key texts to understanding how Christians *believed* at the time, even mention the Jews, simply stating that Jesus suffered and died "under Pontius Pilate." So, for roughly the first millenium of the Jewish Christian relationship, Jews were seen as essentially a symbol of unbelief, and protected—if only as potential converts. Thus, according to Church doctrine and canonical legislation, Jews were to "be tolerated on humanitarian grounds, and indeed preserved on theological grounds,"[17] unlike pagans whose existence was intolerable within the Christian community.

Medieval canon law even made it an excommunicable offense to do violence against Jews or to disrupt Jewish worship, and the Popes regularly rose to the defense of the Jewish community against persecution. Such legislation was in active force throughout the Middle Ages.[18] The later Middle Ages, however, saw the violence of the Crusaders against the Jews of Europe among other atrocities. While officially condemned, one can, as Leon Poliakov has meticulously traced,[19] discern an escalation of anti-Jewish rhetoric in the wake of these and subsequent massacres (e.g., during the Black Plague), as if the theoretical stakes had to be "upped" to rationalize murders already committed. Likewise, Marc Saperstein, in his incisive foreword to the re-issuance of *The Devil and the Jews*, notes that Trachtenberg's study took him only to the most negative anti-Jewish texts and images, while records of more positive attitudes and communal relations were ignored. This side of the picture too must be included, Saperstein believes, if we are to explain "how it was that the Jews were tolerated at all in Christian countries through the Middle Ages—expelled from one land or another, to be sure, but never driven out of Christendom as a whole, never made the object of a holy war of extermination as was directed against Christian heretics."[20]

So the same term cannot adequately be used to describe New Testament polemics as that appropriate for Patristic polemics, nor between Patristic thought and medieval thought, nor between medieval demonization and modern racist anti-Semitism. Maccoby's first error, then, is to fudge over the vastly complex historical record with a single and singly inappropriate term, "anti-Semitism," projecting back into earlier periods developments proper to later ones.

While rejecting Maccoby's approach, however, as rhetorical "sleight of hand," I would hasten to state that the necessary distinctions in no way exculpate Christians or Christianity from the necessity that faces us, post-Holocaust, of reworking our teaching categories and re-thinking the anti-Jewish theological accretions that have grown alongside doctrinal proclamations. Blurring distinctions, however, as Maccoby does, will not be helpful to this crucial and ongoing process.

Cosmic Drama and Christian Doctrine

The Middle Ages saw, among other events, one which I believe has great pertinence to the present considerations. This is the development, in the thirteenth century, of the Passion play.[21] It is here, I feel, that one *can* find something resembling Maccoby's otherwise unrecognizable version of "the Christian myth of redemption." Certainly, the "cosmic drama" he portrays so vividly is not found as such in the New Testament (though various New Testament strands do feed into it) nor in the Creeds, as we have seen, nor in the great syntheses of Christian theology. There, the real "culprit" in Jesus' death is clearly the sins of all humanity. (In Revelations it is, variously, Rome and/or demonic spiritual powers.) The official Roman Catechism of the sixteenth century Council of Trent strongly rebuts those who—perhaps from viewing Passion plays?—would hold such a myth as Maccoby would ascribe to Christian doctrine as such:

> In this guilt are involved all those who fall frequently into sin; for, as our sins consigned Christ the Lord to the death of the cross, most certainly those who wallow in sin and iniquity crucify to themselves again the Son of God, as far in them lies, and make a mockery of him. This guilt seems more enormous in us than in the Jews, since according to the testimony of the same apostle: If they had known it, they would never have crucified the Lord of glory; while we, on the contrary, professing to know him, yet denying him by our actions, seem in some sort to lay violent hands on him (*Heb.* 6:6, 1 *Cor.* 2:8).

This passage also clarifies the proper Christian attitude toward the dynamics of "shifting guilt and responsibility" evoked by Maccoby.

In passion plays one can find (as one cannot in the New Testament itself) Judas functioning as the "epynomous representative of the Jewish people." And one can see how people could come away from such plays with feelings about Jews as "the sacrificers of God."

Christian theology has developed over the centuries several ways, doctrinally and liturgically, of articulating the meaning of Jesus' death and Resurrection. The *Epistle to the Hebrews*, one of the most "anti-Judaic" of the New Testament, for example utilizes the biblical (not pagan) notion of sacrifice, seeing Jesus as at once victim and executioner, offerer and offered, priest-sacrificer and sácrifice. Christ's self-sacrifice, for the author, thus replaces the Temple cult itself as the means of redemption from sin. But even this "substitutionary" theology does not require Jews to act as "sacred executioner." That point is irrelevant, theologically, to the New Testament author's apologetic.

Other New Testament authors draw on various images and themes from the Jewish tradition to describe the Incarnation/Redemption, such as the Passover (Jesus as Paschal Lamb) and sacrifice as *free* human response of humanity-in-Christ to God's universal call to covenantal obedience. Jesus is also variously imaged (typology) as perfect manna, as the suffering of Isaac in the Akedah, as the "new Adam," etc. Several of these images were used to imply that Christ replaces or "perfects" the Jewish models drawn upon. None requires Maccoby's version of the cosmic drama to function symbolically. New Testament soteriology, then, is by no means as simple—or simplistic—as Maccoby's thesis requires.[22]

Maccoby, then, is simply wrong both in his description of "the Christian myth" and in his interpretation of it. "Deicide," while popularly held—even among bishops and theologians—has never been an official Catholic teaching, since it represents a denial of the Incarnation, a form of Docetism early condemned as heresy and bitterly fought by the Church. Jesus, freely and wholly embracing humanity even unto death and responding as man to God, frees humanity from the shackles of sin, making possible and enabling a "new creation," which is to say a new relationship between God and all of humanity. This is the core of the redemptive drama. God is not killed; nor *can* he be killed from a Christian, which is to say, monotheistic point of view. Jesus as human is killed, and as human ("flesh" and all[23]) is raised to glory. Thus there is no need in Christian doctrine for "God-killers."

Maccoby's scenario is not only alien to authentic Christianity, it represents in fact a series of heresies specifically condemned by the Church over the centuries: Docetism, gnosticism, cosmic dualism, etc. For Maccoby to attempt to posit onto Christian doctrine a set of beliefs Christian tradition has already measured and rejected (some very painfully) is both fruitless and it must be said, theologically arrogant. His theory is not adequate to the complexities of Christian doctrine. Though his critique of the function in the popular mind of such phenomena as Passion plays can at times be devastatingly accurate, a grasp of authentic Christian tradition is lacking in his presentation.

This is not to say that Christians do not need to look at the entire corpus of Christian thought in the wake of Auschwitz. All Christian doctrine must today be given the most searching scrutiny in the light of the flames of the crematoria. I and many others have urged this before, and the present Pope has, in a remarkable series of statements, sketched a theological framework for this effort. But Maccoby's thesis, which appears unable to distinguish between a Passion play and a dogma, can only confuse the real issues.

Of Maccoby's list of four areas, two have already been tackled effectively precisely through dialogical theology and the official Church statements Maccoby eschews. The other two, the Incarnation (Maccoby's phrase, "the deification of Jesus" is not a recognizable one in a Christian context) and atonement (which is part of a much larger nexus of theological formulations and concepts and cannot be taken in isolation from these as Maccoby's theory demands) are not, properly understood, at issue.

Maccoby's thesis, in sum, cannot be taken seriously. He has invented his own personal version of Christianity in order to denounce it. The polemical technique he uses, sadly, is a familiar one. Ironically, it was perfected by

Christians in erecting the corrupt edifice of the teaching of contempt against Jews and Judaism. My own hunch is that perhaps Maccoby does not, in a sense, wish to be taken seriously. Little else would explain his studied ignorance of actual Christian tradition. Perhaps he simply wishes us to understand the experience from the other side.

Maccoby has produced, not a scholarly thesis, or a contribution to the understanding of the origins of anti-Semitism, as the title of this conference portends. He has produced an inversion of the Christian polemic, a carefully constructed satire on our own worst foibles. As satire, i.e., as fiction, it may find its proper place on the library shelves and could be salutory for the Christian reader who understands its true nature. It enables us to laugh at ourselves while laughing with him. But it remains fiction in the literary form of an extremely vicious polemic. It should not be confused with fact or interreligious insight.

NOTES

1. Chiefly, Professor Maccoby's summary papers for the present conference and his related articles in *Commentary*: "Gospel and Midrash" (April, 1980) "Theologian of the Holocaust" (Dec., 1982) and "Christianity's Break with Judaism" (August, 1984), along with his responses to readers including myself, in the "Letters" sections of *Commentary* for March 1983 and June 1983.

2. For works produced in the last decade, see my "A New Maturity in Christian-Jewish Dialogue: An Annotated Bibliography 1973-1983." *Face to Face: An Interreligious Bulletin*, Vol. 11, Spring 1984, pp. 29-43. For earlier works see the relevant essays in *The Study of Judaism: Bibliographical Essays*, New York: Anti-Defamation League of B'nai B'rith, 2 Volumes, 1974, 1976.

3. Eugene Fisher, "Typical Jewish Misunderstandings of Christianity," *Judaism*, Spring, 1973, pp. 21-32.

4. See Helga Croner, *Stepping Stones to Further Christian-Jewish Relations*, London: Stimulus, 1977, currently being updated, for both Protestant and Catholic documents, for publication in 1985 by Paulist Press.

5. *Nostra Aetate*, no. 4 has been criticized for failing to use the words "deicide" and "condemn." What it said was that "what happened in his passion cannot be charged against all the Jews, without distinction, then alive, nor against the Jews of today." Since the statement rebuts any sense of collective responsibility of the Jews for Jesus' death on straightforward grounds (it is not stated as an exoneration but a simple matter of historical and theological truth) there can be no question of a "deicide" charge, and, in fact, the word has entirely disappared from Roman Catholic catechisms. Regarding "condemn," this was removed because of Pope John XXIII's wish that the Council, unlike previous councils, present positive teaching and avoid all sense of "anathema." Interestingly, the word "condemn" is used twice in the section of the 1974 Vatican "Guidelines and Suggestions for Implementing the Conciliar Declaration, *Nostra Aetate*, no. 4" which "restates" the declaration. A major problem with Maccoby's responses to my own comments on his theories (*Commentary*, March, June, 1983) is that, in approaching the Council he fails to take into account its official interpretation in subsequent documents. Thus, he comes up with interpretations which are contrary to its intent and spirit. Such errors can be avoided by reference to the relevant official statements.

6. The normative value of this statement within a Catholic understanding of Tradition is carefully presented in Jorge Mejia, "A Christian View of Bible Interpretation," in *Biblical Studies: Meeting Ground of Jews and Christians*, edited by L. Boadt, H. Croner, and L. Klenicki, New York: Paulist Press, Stimulus Boods, pp. 45-72). Cf. esp. pp. 60 and 71.

7. Tommaso, Federici, "Study Outline on the Mission and Witness of the Church," *SIDIC*, Rome, Vol. 11, no. 3, 1978, pp. 25-34.

8. John Paul II, Address to American Jewish Committee representatives, Feb. 15, 1985.

9. Cf. John G. Gager, *The Origins of Anti-Semitism: Attitudes Toward Judaism in Pagan and Christian Antiquity*, New York: Oxford University Press, 1983, pp. 13-34; and John T. Pawlikowski, *What Are They Saying About Christian-Jewish Relations?* New York: Paulist Press, 1980, for illuminating summaries of this literature.

10. Alan T. Davies, *Anti-Semitism and the Foundations of Christianity*, New York: Paulist Press, 1980, p. xv.

11. Samuel Sandmel, *Anti-Semitism in the New Testament?* Philadelphia: Fortress, 1978, p. xxi, though Sandmel continues to use the term because the "correct" terms (anti-Jewish, anti-Judaism) "simply have not caught on."

12. This can be seen in the opposition to the Nazi roundups of *baptised* Jews even by otherwise pro-Nazi and anti-Semitic Christian clergy.

13. John G. Gager, *The Origins of Anti-Semitism, op. cit.*

14. Robert L. Wilken, *John Chrysostum and the Jews: Rhetoric and Reality in the Late 4th Century*, Los Angeles: University of California Press, 1983, see esp. p. 164.

15. Second paperback reissued for the Anti-Defamation League of B'nai B'rith by JPS in 1983.

16. Raul Hilberg in *The Destruction of European Jews* cites as a first instance the burning of the Talmud by the 12th Synod of Toledo in 681 of the Common Era (p. 5). Cf. J. E. Scherer, *Die Rechtsverhältnisse der deutschöterriechischen Ländern* (Leipzig, 1901), pp. 39-49.

17. Trachtenberg, *Devil*, p. 164.

18. See Edward A. Synan, *The Popes and the Jews in the Middle Ages*, New York: Macmillan, 1965.

19. Leon Poliakov, *The History of Anti-Semitism*, New York: Schoken, 1974.

20. Marc Saperstein, "Foreword" to 1983 Edition of Trachtenberg, p. ix. Saperstein notes (p. xi) as well a methodological flaw in Trachtenberg's approach that also mars Maccoby's reconstruction of history: "Trachtenberg drew two apparently conflicting conclusions. Where official Church policy was favorable to the Jews, it was unimportant: 'It is of no point that the Church did not directly charge the Jew *qua* heretic, with such abominable anti-Christian practices. What matters is that the common people and their clerical mentors made the association' (p. 207). But where policy was unfavorable to the Jews, it was more important than any of the political, social and economic transformations of medieval society in the twelfth and thirteenth centuries, for all these 'operated against the backdrop of Church policy, which determined public opinion. . . and which must in the end bear the major responsibility for the transformation of the popular attitude toward the Jew' (p. 161)."

21. See Eugene Fisher and Leon Klenicki, "Parish Passion Plays: What Do They Teach?" *PACE* 15, St. Mary's Press, Feb. 1985, "Issues - B," p. 2.

22. On New Testament soteriology within the context of passion plays, see L. Swidler and G. Sloyan, "The Passion of the Jew Jesus:

Recommended Chages in the Oberammergau Passion Play After 1984," in *Face to Face*, New York, Anti-Defamation League, vol. 12, Winter 1985, p. 33. They state: "All Christians have the conviction that the obedient sacrifice of Jesus on the cross atoned perfectly for the sins of all humanity. This conviction is found most fully expressed in the epistles of *St. Paul*. Even there, however, *no complete and consistent soteriology is to be found (i.e., a theology of salvation or redemption)*. In the gospels such a soteriology is even more elusive. The evangelists content themselves with phrases like, "to give his life as a ransom for the many," "the lamb of God who takes away the sins of the world," and "this is my blood of the covenant to be poured out for the many for the forgiveness of sins." *"At no time does any of the four set his narrative of Jesus' sufferings and death in a context of the purpose of that death. Phrases like those above, which fall outside the arrest and crucifixion accounts, represent as much reflection on the mystery as the evangelists allow themselves.* Consequently, the play does well to present scenes intended to excite the viewers' sympathy for the suffering just one (for that is what the evangelists did); but it needs to be very careful about the theology of redemption it supplies from a later time."

23. The emphasis in the Patristic theology of the Eucharist upon the bread and wine as truly Jesus' "flesh and blood" is properly understood as an insulation against gnosticism and its dualistic tendencies. The doctrine of the Incarnation, the belief that Christ is at once "fully human and fully God" binds together the spiritual and earthly "realms" which gnostic dualism would see as wholly separated. This central Christian belief, then, becomes *the* battleground between orthodoxy and the gnostic heterodoxies of the Patristic period. On the key function of Eucharistic theology in this debate (won creedally by orthodoxy), see Alastair I. C. Heron, *Table and Tradition: Toward an Ecumenical Understanding the Eucharist*. Philadelphia: Westminster Press, 1983, pp. 59-67, *et passim*. Heron also sees anti-gnosticism as a motivation behind the shift in language in the institution narratives from the earlier narratives from "This is the new covenant in my blood" to "This is my blood of the covenant." The earlier narratives drew upon the covenant-theology of the Servant Songs of *Isaiah* 42, 49, 52-53, Heron states, while the latter focus more on the covenant theology of *Exodus* 24:5-8 (cf. pp. 9-16). It is only with the latter theology that the Eucharist is seen as a "sacrifice." The earlier Eucharistic theory does not depend on sacrifice for its understanding of the Christ-Event.

A Reply to Hyam Maccoby's
The Sacred Executioner
Rev. Robert Andrew Everett

Professor Maccoby's thesis, as reflected in his *The Sacred Executioner*, and his articles on anti-Semitism have been quite thought provoking. He has raised some issues about the relationship of Christianity to anti-Semitism which I had not considered before now. I have no disagreement with him on the point that Christianity has indeed been the major source of anti-Jewish thought in Western culture. Even given the obvious difference between Nazi racial theory and Christian doctrine, one must still recognize the connection between the success of the Nazi anti-Jewish program and the environment created for such policies by the long history of Christian hatred of the Jews. It is irrefutable that the Holocaust had its genesis in the heart of Christian Europe, in that most Christian of states, Germany. One cannot ignore the continual influence of Christian teaching, iconography and calendar thinking in Europe, even in the nineteenth century when secularization made great headway, and racial theories, which denied the kinship of men and women to the One God, were being developed. The Holocaust was made possible because the Church had indeed made Jews a ready target for a political movement like Nazism.

It is a bit of intellectual hubris to point to the Enlightenment as the source of modern European culture, particularly as regards popular opinion. The idea that Christianity and its symbols became a secondary power in this period may be correct in so far as the salons of Paris were concerned. But I am not so sure that Voltaire really was such a great influence beyond the salons. Christianity continued to have a powerful hold over the hearts and minds of the mass of common folk throughout Europe, and it was

Christianity which continued to supply the popular imagination with the negative image of the Jews, which in turn enabled those who held non-Christian or anti-Christian anti-Semitic positions to succeed in singling out the Jews as the common enemy of the people. This was, of course, crucial in their attempt to make political and economic anti-Semitism acceptable to the masses. Herein lies an important link between Christian teachings and the Nazi Holocaust. In his study of nineteenth century French anti-Semitism, Robert Byrnes points out that during the second half of the century the strength of the French anti-Semitic Catholic movement lay "in the provinces, untouched by the cosmopolitan and intellectual developments of the capital."[1] It was the Church which continued to be a seedbed of anti-Jewish thought for the general populace.

It is also singularly incorrect to contrast racial anti-Semitism as if one had nothing to do with the other. The work of the late Uriel Tal of Tel Aviv University is most helpful in showing how racialist theory and Christianity were often strange bedfellows.[2] Many of the racialists did not want to give up their Christianity, and they either alleged that Christ was an Aryan/Teuton or they merely appealed to the Macionist idea that the God of the Hebrew Bible was really the Devil or an evil godling. The racists did argue against the efficacy of baptism for Jews because they did not believe that baptism could in any way change Jewish blood, thus, even converted Jews remained Jews in their eyes. However, the questioning of the efficacy of baptism for Jews was not an original idea of the racists. Luther questioned the same in 1539. The connection between pure blood and Christian faith can also be found in the debates in Spain over the Marranoes. *Limpios* became a distinguishing feature of the Old Christians vs. the New Christians.[3] Looking at the development of the racist theories, one also finds that the most successful efforts were those which "displayed a readiness to reconcile themselves to be continued existence of Christianity on the condition that it substitute the biological values of the Aryan race for its Jewish origins." Thus, Jesus became an Aryan in the writing of Houston Stewart Chamberlain and the "Deutsche Christian" Church of the Third Reich. So while I believe that racism is absolutely incompatible with Christianity, it is not the case that racist ideas about Jesus are totally foreign to the Christian tradition despite the fact that such an idea is really alien to the essence of Christian faith. But to try to use secularization, the Enlightenment, or racism as reasons why Christianity played no role in the development of the Holocaust and modern anti-Semitism is, to my mind, impossible. We must face the awful truth that there is a most deadly relationship which cannot be ignored. Intellectual honesty demands no less.

Now I raise these points in order to establish that Christians should not be overly defensive about some of the charges Dr. Maccoby raises. He is well within his rights, and I would add, his duty, to issue this indictment. Where I tend to have some questions about his theory is in his use of the myth of the Sacred Executioner to draw his argument. I fear that such an approach is both full of possibilities and fraught with ambiguity. It may be my own uneasiness with psycho-history as an intellectual method that leads me to this position. While I think he clearly has raised new evidence about the roots of Christian anti-Semitism, the esoteric nature of his thesis may prove too abstract to have any concrete influence on Christian attitudes toward Jews. This is really a pragmatic argument because I think the substance of Maccoby's position is quite sound. I would prefer, however, to argue for a position which exposes what I call the "theology of victimization" which has characterized the Christian theological view of Jews and Judaism. Much in this position echoes Dr. Maccoby, but I believe that it attacks the problem on a more historical-political level, and is open to a more possible, although by no means assured, reinterpretation of Christian theology. It also allows one to deal specifically with the question of Christian anti-Zionism as a continuation of its theology of victimization. Allow me to clarify my position.

It is distressing to say, but true nevertheless, that Christians have historically viewed Jews only as victims. In fact, this ideological view of Jews as victims has been supported by a Christian theology of victimization; a theology that appeared to give divine sanction to the belief that Jews were fated to be eternal victims.

The theology of the victimization of the Jewish people is an idea deeply rooted in Christian theology. The basis of this theology forms what Jules Isaac has called the "teaching of contempt."[4] The theology of victimization took hold in Christian thought when the early church leveled the charge of deicide against the Jewish people. The charge is found in the Gospels and in the writings of Paul.[5] The alleged role of the Jews in the death of Jesus, and their rejection of the Church's claim that he was the Messiah of Israel were used as grounds to justify the idea that God had cursed the Jewish people. According to Church teachings, all Jews were under this curse for all time. Their only chance for redemption was by conversion to Christianity, and Jews who remained Jews remained cursed. The idea that the Jews are a cursed people deeply embedded itself in Christian thought, and it has had a very lively history and a powerful hold on the Christian mind. Until recently, it was almost impossible to find any Christian thinker who thought otherwise, and the idea certainly informed popular opinion among Christians.

Perhaps one of the most jolting examples of how this theme has survived in the Christian mind comes from a most unexpected source, Dietrich Bonhoeffer. Bonhoeffer was able to write that "the Church of Christ has never lost sight of the thought that the 'chosen people' who nailed the redeemer of the world to the cross must bear the curse of its action through the long history of suffering."[6] Bonhoeffer, the great Christian martyr of the Nazi era, sums up perfectly the whole attitude of the Christian tradition toward Jews. They are victims of a divine curse. This theological idea has made Christians rather indifferent to Jewish suffering. As Bonhoeffer explains, Jews suffer because they killed Jesus and rejected him as Messiah. The early

Church believed they had historical validation for this theology. Hadn't the Temple been destroyed in 70 C.E.? Were not the Jews dispersed from the Land at that time? Wasn't this a clear sign of God's displeasure? The Church answered in the affirmative to these questions, and thus solidified within its theological tradition a theology of victimization of the Jewish people.[7] As the Church gained political power, it was able to translate its theology into political and social policy.[8] The theological accursedness of the Jews manifested itself in Christian laws which made Jews outcasts and victims of Christian hostility and power. The Jewish experience in Christendom has been characterized by forced baptism, expulsion, and death.[9]

An important component of the Christian theology of victimization is the idea that Jews are in total exile: exile from God, exile from their supposed Savior, and exile from their land. All of Jewish history and Jewish reality was interpreted as an exile. The legend of the Wandering Jew personified the belief that Jews were both historically and ontologically in exile. In Christian thought, they were shadow figures who were a dire warning of the consequences of unbelief and a people devoid of any means of redemption. A whole tradition sprang from the theology of victimization which linked the Jews to the Devil.[10] This mythology did much to reinforce the notion that Christians should be suspicious of Jews, and that Jews deserved any suffering inflicted upon them. It made perfect sense to believe that if Jews were cursed and rejected by God, they would naturally hate God and be willing to serve the Devil, the Archenemy of God. No crime was too horrendous to accuse the Jews of committing. It became commonplace to believe that Jews killed Christian children for their blood, that they poisoned wells and that they desecrated the Eucharistic host. Wasn't that simply a replay of the original deicide? The more Jews were demonized, the easier it was to justify their status as victims. They deserved it, according to Christian theology.

According to the theology of victimization, it was out of the question that Jews could ever regain their sovereignty over the Land of Israel. Historically, it isn't true that Jews were totally exiled from the Land. Jews have always lived in the Land since the time of Jesus.[11] Christians, however, firmly believed in the idea that the Jewish diaspora was a direct result of their divine punishment. Theologically, it appeared impossible for Jews to ever regain sovereignty of the Land. Sovereignty would imply Jewish power, and Jews as victims, according to Christian theology, were not allowed to have power. When Pope Pius X told Theodor Herzl that the Church could not accept the Jews repossessing the Holy Land as long as they refused to accept Christ, he was merely reiterating the traditional Christian theology of victimization. For the Jews as Jews, there can be no power, no sovereignty, no redemption. They can only be victims.

The theology of victimization also reflects just how powerful an influence the ideas of Marcion have been on the Church. The dramatic dualism in Christian thought that contrasts the Church as the New Israel over against the Jews of the Old Israel, Jewish Law versus Christian Grace, the God of Vengeance of the Old Testament versus the God of Love in the New Testament all reflect Marcionist tendencies. The supersessionist theology of the Church, which claims that all the promises of God now belong to the Church while God's curses belong to Israel, is a major factor in the theology of victimization. Judaism and the Jewish people came to have no real value for Christians except as a negative contrast to Christianity. While Marcion was branded finally as a heretic, his basic thesis of separating the Church from Israel was ultimately incorporated into the Church's teachings.[12] Even the continued use of the term Old Testament by Christians to refer to the Hebrew Bible is a subtle indication of a mindset unable to see anything positive in Judaism.[13] Christian theology has been able to deal with Jews only in negative terms. Christian apologetics claim the God of Abraham, Isaac, and Jacob as their own, but it has insisted that "what begins in the one is consummated in the other, what starts with the one is fulfilled in the other, and the darkly perceived and imperfect God of the Jews is transfigured and illuminated by the God of Christian love and grace. . . . Marcionism was repudiated as having indited an absolute theological ceasura, but the Marcionist suspicion and loathing for the dark God of creation and the Jews is preserved as the teaching of the humiliation of the Jews."[14] Ultimately, the Church's triumphalistic theology could be justified only by making the Jews its most obvious victims.

The theology of victimization of the Jews raises grave moral problems for Christianity. Upon immediate reflection, it seems that the Christian ethic of love would be a potent antidote for such an idea. But the theology of victimization proves quite immune to Christian love. Once it is established that God has cursed the Jews, how can one then argue that Christians should love them? If Jews have been fated by God to have, as Bonhoeffer said, a long history of suffering, who are Christians to try to alter this history by doing anything to relieve Jewish suffering? The theology of victimization thus precludes Christian love as a basis for relating to Jews. Their role as victim is divinely ordained. Traditionally, it has been believed that the only love Christians could show Jews is by converting them, but that is nothing but a less violent form of victimization which still denies Jews any hope of redemption or divine love while they remain Jews. It is really a form of spiritual genocide against the Jewish people.

During the Holocaust, Jews became the ultimate victims. Jews alone were singled out for complete extermination.[15] For Christians who follow the theology of victimization to its logical conclusion, the Holocaust raises no moral problems. But can we really accept the idea that our theology justifies such a victimization of the Jews? Does not the continued acceptance of a theology of victimization make us accomplices in the murder of the Jews? Christians today have proven willing to deal with the problems of theological racism, sexism, and sexual oppression. Are we not called

today, in light of the Holocaust, to reconsider our theology
of the victimization of the Jews?

The Catholic theologian David Tracy has suggested that
an hermeneutics of suspicion be applied to the Christian
theological tradition.[17] Such an hermeneutics may discover
that "later historical events can demand reinterpretations
of the founding events. Indeed, later historical events can
even challenge not the founding religious event but the authoritative response to that event."[18] The Holocaust demands of Christians that they apply this hermeneutics of
suspicion to their theology of victimization. The Church
stands condemned for the social and political consequences
of its ideology of victimization in the Holocaust. In light
of the Holocaust, it is a moral imperative that the Church
reinterpret this theology so that it is no longer implicated
in the crime of theologically supporting the victimization
of the Jewish people. This imperative leads us directly to
Zionism and the State of Israel and their meaning for
Christians and Christian theology.

The redemptive nature of Zionism in Jewish life cannot
be underestimated. Zionism has allowed the Jew once
again to claim such universal ideas as justice, truth, and
peace within his or her particular Jewish identity. Zionism
is the revival of Jewish Messianic hopes, giving new meaning to Jewish life and history. Zionism has lifted the Jews
out of the state of victimization and given them power.
With this power, Jews are now able to resist any attempt
to make them victims. Liberation theology has no better
model for the implementation of its goals than Zionism.[19]

With their return to history as a sovereign nation, Jews
have now put an end to the myth of exile. Theologically
interpreted, Zionism is the fulfillment of God's promise to
His people that they would have a land in which to live as
people, and that land is Israel. Zionism belies the theological idea that the Jews are a cursed people. With the re-
emergence of a sovereign Jewish state, one is faced with
the historical fulfillment of the divine promise. The State
of Israel can be interpreted as a holy reality for Jews as it

is the most viisble and concrete symbol of God's unending grace and love for His people.[20] The State of Israel may well be of sacramental significance for Christians as well. It is, to be sure, a very mundane and historical sacrament, but a symbol of redemption nonetheless.[21]

The theology of victimization of the Jewish people has been employed by Christians to justify their belief that Jews should be victims for nearly two thousand years. But this theology really has been a cancer in the soul of Christianity. It made a mockery of Christian love. It permitted Christians to ignore the evil consequences of its theological tradition. It compromised the Church as a moral agent. It deformed the Christian character. It ultimately involved the Christian community in the attempted genocide of the Jewish people. This long accepted theology of victimization now has turned on Christians as an accuser. Christians stand accused of being victimizers by consequence of their own theological beliefs. The very credibility of the Christian enterprise is now challenged by how Christians respond to their accuser.

The overwhelming evidence against Christians as the victimizers of the Jewish people would seem to preclude any possible acquittal of the charges. But the judge in this case is God, and because God is the judge, there is hope. According to a rabbinic story, when a person is judged by God, God sits upon the seat of judgment. But when God goes to pass sentence, He sits upon the seat of mercy.[22] Despite the crimes committed in the name of the theology of victimization, Christians have been extended the divine hand of mercy through Zionism. Christians who wish to redeem themselves and their theological tradition from the role of victimizers of the Jewish people can do so by supporting the Zionist effort to restore power to the Jewish people and to free them from being victims. Christians can receive God's grace only by supporting His continual love and redemption of the Jewish people demonstrated in the restoration of Israel. By their support of Zionism and the State of Israel, Christians take the first step in freeing themselves from the theology of victimization. The anti-Zionism found in the Christian Church today is simply the proof that the theology of victimization has not been completely overcome. Anti-Zionist Christians still see Jews only as victims and never as victors within human history. Christian anti-Zionism is a denial of God's grace to both Christians and Jews.

Zionism has overturned the theology of victimization. The Christian claims that Jews are a cursed people is belied by the restoration of Jewish sovereignty over the Land of Israel. The long history of Christian victimization of the Jews has now made Christians victims of their own self-inflicted sin. Christian resistance to the Jewish state will continue as long as Christians are unable to overcome the theological prejudice which says Jews are to be victims. Until we do overcome, until we are able to support and defend the Jewish State, we Christians will remain tied to a theological tradition which justifies our playing a role in victimizing the Jewish people. But history has now transformed our faith. It is ironic that those considered victims for so long should now be the sourse of Christian redemption. This wouldn't be the first time, however, that salvation has come from the Jews.[23] It is no longer necessary to believe that in order to love Jesus we must make his people victims and hate them. Zionism is not only an instrument of redemption for Jews, but can now be seen as having a redemptive quality for Christians, freeing them from being victimizers. How we choose to respond to Zionism will determine whether we live in grace or sin.

My only problem with Maccoby, and it is a minor one, is that his position on the theology of victimization, as I have presented it, may be too ideational. It is not a myth that Jews have been victims, often at the hands of the Church, rather it is a fact with a concrete history. It is a myth, however, that they should be victims. Maccoby has done much to show where the roots of that myth lie in Christian thought. But a myth based on a lie is not a myth but a lie. A profoundly simple thought, but one often ignored. And when that is the case, the myth loses all its mythic value. The Jews did not crucify Jesus. Christians can only overcome that myth/lie when they are finally willing to accept historical facts which show that only the Romans could have carried out such a punishment. Once that fact is accepted by the Church, it will no longer need a theology of victimization of the Jewish people. Maccoby is correct in pointing out the mythic roots of this theology, and I must backtrack a bit from my initial comments about his position creating more problems than it solves. It needs to be seen that Maccoby's position is a quite logical one given the traditional view of the Church concerning Jews. Again, I may simply be arguing a pragmatic position which in no way detracts from Maccoby's work. It is a fact that historical facts often pale before theological speculation. In this sense, Maccoby may be correct in attacking the problem on mythological grounds.

I do think that Dr. Maccoby's theory does challenge the Christian world to do some serious theological thinking about its understanding of Jesus and the meaning of his death. A Christology based on a lie would still be a lie. This we cannot have. Maccoby is helpful in pointing out some of the dangers inherent in some of Christianity's traditional thought. The validity of a theology must be judged by not only its content, but on its social and political ramifications. I thank Dr. Maccoby for challenging the Christian community to once again deal with both the theory and praxis of its theology concerning Jesus. After the Holocaust, this must be a top priority of the Church.

NOTES

1. Robert Byrnes, *Antisemitism in Modern France*. New Brunswick, New Jersey: Rutgers Press, 1950, p. 187.

2. Uriel Tal, *Christians and Jews in Germany: Religion, Politics and Ideology in the Second Reich 1870-1914*. Ithaca and London: Cornell Press, 1975.

3. Leon Poliakov, *The History of Antisemitism*. Vol. II. New York: Vanguard Press, 1975, pp. 224-25.

4. Jules Isaac, *The Teaching of Contempt: Christian Roots of Antisemitism.* New York: Holt, Rinehart and Wilson, 1964.

5. See *Matthew* 27: 11-26; *Mark* 14: 1, 11, 43ff, 55, 64 and 15: 11-15; *Luke* 23: 1-25; and *John* 19: 1-16; Act 2: 22-24; 1st Thess. 2: 14-16. See two important books on the whole question of the role Jews played in the death of Jesus: Haim Cohn, *The Trial and Death of Jesus.* New York: Harper & Row, 1967; Paul Winter, *On the Trial of Jesus.* Berlin: Walter De Gruyer & Co., 1961. For the impact of the deicide charge on Christian theology see: James Parkes, *Conflict of the Church and Synagogue.* London: The Soncino Press, 1934; Rosemary Ruether, *Faith and Fratricide.* New York: Seabury Press, 1974; Leon Poliakov, *The History of Antisemitism.* New York: Vanguard Press, 1975; Franklin Littell, *The Crucifixion of the Jews.* New York: Harper & Row, 1975; A. Roy Eckardt, *Your People, My People.* New York: Quadrangle Books, 1974, pp. 3-42; John T. Pawlikowski, *What Are They Saying About Christian-Jewish Relations?* New York: Paulist Press, 1980, pp. 1-33.

6. Dietrich Bonhoeffer, *No Rusty Swords.* London: Collins, The Fontana Library, 1970, p. 222.

7. On the Patristic Literature see: James Parkes, *The Conflict of Church and Synagogue*, Chapter Five. A. Lukyn Williams, *Adversos Judaeos.* Cambridge, Cambridge University Press, 1935. Rosemary Ruether, *op. cit.*, Chapter Three. The intensity of the hatred shown Jews in the writings of the Fathers is matched only by their writings on women. See Friedrich Heer, *God's First Love.* London: Weybright and Tally, 1967, pp. 38-50.

8. See James Parkes, *The Jew in the Medieval Community: A Study in His Political and Economic Situation.* London: The Soncino Press, 1938. Leon Poliakov, *op. cit.*, Vol. II & III; Solomon Grayzel, *The Church and the Jews in the XII Century.* New York: Harman Press, 1966. Rosemary Ruether, *op. cit.*, pp. 183-226. Edward Synan, *The Popes and the Jews in the Middle Ages.* New York: Macmillan, 1965.

9. Raul Hilberg, *The Destruction of the European Jews.* New York: Quadrangle Books, 1967, pp. 1-17. See particularly pages 5-6 for a comparison of Canonical Laws with Nazi measures against Jews.

10. Joshua Trachenburg, *The Devil and the Jews.* New Haven: Yale University Press, 1943, is an excellent study of the tradition.

11. See Parkes, *Whose Land?* and Joan Peters, *From Time Immemorial.* New York: Harper & Row, 1983, for accounts of the Jewish presence in the Land.

12. Arthur A. Cohen points out that Marcion's desire to "set up a counter-Church bound by. . . strict rules of asceticism" may have been the real reason he was ultimately rejected as a heretic, not his views on the Jews. See: Arthur A. Cohen, "The Holocaust and Christian Theology: An Interpretation of the Problem" in *Judaism and*

Christianity Under the Impact of National-Socialism. Jerusalem: The Historical Society of Israel, 1982, footnote 19, p. 439.

13. John Pawlikowski, "Jews and Christians: The Contemporary Debate." *Quarterly Review*, 4, no. 4 Winter 1984, pp. 26-27.

14. Cohen, *op. cit.*, pp. 424-425, footnote 6.

15. On the question of the uniqueness of the Holocaust see: Steven Katz, *Post-Holocaust Dialogues: Critical Studies in Modern Jewish Thought.* New York: NYU Press, 1983, pp. 287-319; A. Roy and Alice Eckardt, *Long Night's Journey Into Day: Life and Faith After the Holocaust.* Detroit: Wayne State Press, 1982, pp. 41-66; Emil Fackenheim, *To Mend the World.* New York: Schocken Books, 1982, pp. 9-14.

16. A recent statement by the World Council of Churches meeting in Vancouver, B.C. that urged Christians not to allow the Holocaust to be a factor in how they viewed the Arab-Israel conflict reflects the Church's tendency to ignore the history of Jewish victimization at the hands of Christians. The W.C.C.'s position can only be described as morally bankrupt. It is as if the W.C.C. told whites in America to ignore the history of Black slavery in American history when trying to understand the Black condition today or telling men not to think about the history of male sexism when deciding upon feminist issues.

17. David Tracy, "Religious Values after the Holocaust" in *Christians and Jews After the Holocaust*, Abraham Peck, ed. Philadelphia: Fortress Press, 1980, pp. 87-110.

18. As quoted in Cohen, *op. cit.*, footnote 6, p. 436. See also footnotes 3, 4, and 8, pp. 435-437. I am indebted to Cohen's insights on the application of Tracy's hermeneutics of suspicion to the question of theology and the Holocaust and the issue of Zionism.

19. John T. Pawlikowski, *Christ in the Light of the Christian-Jewish Dialogue.* New York/Ramsey: Paulist Press, 1982, pp. 59-75 contains an interesting survey of how Liberation theologians deal and do not deal with issues of Jewish-Christian relations and Zionism.

20. Tal, "Jewish Self-Understanding and the Land and State of Israel," *Union Seminary Quarterly Review*, New York, vol. 26, no. 4, Summer 1971, for ways in which Jewish thinkers have dealt with this problem, particularly the ideas of Abraham Isaac Kook.

21. A. Roy Eckardt, "Secular Theology of Israel." *Christian-Jewish Relations*, London: no. 72, Sept. 1980.

22. C. G. Montefiore and H. Loewe, *A Rabbinic Anthropology.* New York: Schocken Press, 1974, p. 234. *Lev. R.* Emor, xxix, 3.

23. *John* 4:22. The hostility of the writer of John's Gospel toward the Jews remains problematic for contemporary Jewish-Christian relations. On this point, of salvation coming from the Jews, the writer may have unwittingly given us a profound truth that Christians have forgotten all too often.

A Response to Professor Hyam Maccoby
Rabbi A. James Rudin

Professor Hyam Maccoby is an original thinker in the field of religious history. He has consistently developed and advanced new, even radical ideas, and by so doing, he has compelled others to stretch their minds and to think of novel answers to age old questions. Whether one agrees or disagrees with Professor Maccoby, we are in his debt for presenting us with innovative approaches to well trod areas of scholarly inquiry.

Like so many other Christians and Jews, Maccoby is obsessed with the pernicious and bloody results of Christian anti-Semitism. Like all of us, he clearly recognizes that we are dealing with a persistent and virulent form of social pathology, and like a serious scientist, Maccoby attempts to locate the cause of the illness, to isolate out the cause from a plethora of offered explanations. Ultimately, it is his hope to eradicate the deathly pathology. It is a commendable goal, worthy of our respect and our thanks.

Staggered by the incredible suffering that Christian anti-Semitism has caused, Maccoby suggests a startling thesis to explain this devastating pathology: the "Sacred Executioner" myth. In effect, Maccoby identifies the cause of Christian anti-Semitism in quasi mythical terms; the need for human sacrifice, and the guilt and anger that is placed upon the person or persons who are forced to commit these heinous, but necessary acts. Maccoby suggests the Jewish people sacrificed a fellow Jew, Jesus of Nazareth, as part of a carefully orchestrated ritual, and thus the Jews, singly and collectively, have incurred the wrath of Christians and Christianity ever since. Because the cause of Christian anti-Semitism is deeply embedded in a subconscious myth, Maccoby is highly pessimistic about the efficacy of what he terms "cosmetic excisions" of troublesome New Testament passages, and he is equally pessimistic about "exhortations to recognition of Judaism (by Christians) as an independent religion, much as these measures are to be welcomed." Maccoby urges us to go far beyond these insufficient steps.

But where does Maccoby's thesis lead us and leave us? If he is correct, that the locus of the disease is a deep seated myth, how does he propose to treat it? What cures does he offer? It seems to me he has led us into a Freudian forest, perhaps even a jungle, where speculation, psychohistorical analysis, and a form of poetic research suggest a primordial act of cosmic importance, the sacred execution of Jesus.

Unfortunately, Maccoby's theory of a primal myth suffers from the same general problem that all such psychoanalytical theories run into: they are simply not provable, not testable by any empirical method of evaluation. All such theories cannot be be proven false, and, of course, they cannot be verified either. So we are left with a far reaching hypothesis that is immune to any rigorous testing that could determine its validity.

While Maccoby's thesis is dramatic, even provocative, I do not believe it is capable of demonstrable proof. This, of course, does not mean that it is not true. I am suggesting that it can not be clearly proven to the degree that it will be universally accepted. Such an acceptance is necessary to enlist the forces needed to exorcise anti-Semitism from Christian consciousness and behavior. But let us for a moment assume that Maccoby is correct, that he has, indeed, isolated out of a myriad of various theories and suggestions the basic cause of Christian anti-Semitism. Let us assume he has, like a gifted medical researcher, isolated the virus, the strain of poison that has produced such extensive human suffering.

Maccoby's recommended cures are aimed at two of the basic foundations of Christianity: "the deification of Jesus and the concept of atonement." He is concerned that Jews have been portrayed in Christianity as "the embodiments of the worst in human nature." Maccoby is also rightly concerned how the myth of alleged Jewish culpability and guilt has been used as a "rationalization" for "post-Christian secular versions of anti-Semitism."

Clearly, Hyam Maccoby thinks in cosmic terms, as indeed we must all do following the tragic and unspeakable end product of Christian anti-Semitism: the Nazi Holocaust. Maccoby is morally correct when he asserts that mere academic speculation is no longer sufficient or acceptable after the Holocaust. Christians and Jews together need to devote enormous energy and skills to a massive campaign to root out the curse of Christian anti-Semitism.

But, alas, I am not certain that Maccoby's approach is the one we should adopt in pursuit of this worthy and necessary objective. I am uneasy with the interpretation offered by the "Sacred Executioner" myth.

Maccoby's attempt to reclaim or better uncover the ancient cause of the cancer is not convincing enough to draw the kind of support that is needed to root out Christian anti-Semitism. His is a poetic, exciting, dramatic, but ultimately unprovable exploration into a dark realm of the human spirit.

All of us employ the best tools of our scholarly craft, as well as our fertile imaginations, to discover what preceded our religious traditions. What, after all, are the primal foundations of the Passover holiday, the ancient foundations that were in place long, long before the Exodus from Egypt? What ancient mythic urges are in the raucous, noisy, and deadly Purim story? What is the "first cause" of the virgin birth story? Our list of such inquiries is almost endless. Maccoby, as indicated earlier, deserves our gratitude for devoting his creative energies to the problem of Christian anti-Semitism.

Yet, strain as we might, the truth is that ultimate "first causes," especiall the kind that would explain anti-Semitism remain beyond our ken, they remain inaccessible. If this is so, and I believe it is, then it will be impossible to tackle the areas that Maccoby has suggested. For Christians to reinterpret, to fundamentally change their historical and

theological view of the divinity of Jesus, demands a purposeful commitment to such a radical and far-reaching change.
I am afraid that Maccoby's thesis is not sufficient to enlist
such widespread and vital support within the Christian
community.

Nor will Maccoby's Sacred Executioner thesis energize
Christian scholars and thinkers to reinterpret the concept
of vicarious atonement. To use a pedestrian expression
borrowed from the world of Madison Avenue advertising,
I am afraid that if Maccoby's mythical explanation were
sent up a flagpole, few would salute it.

Maccoby's original thinking, however, is of importance
in another way. He has forced those who are engaged in
what he has termed "cosmetic excisions" to rethink their
basic assumptions and beliefs. He has probed deeply into
new areas, and even though few of us will probably join
him in his findings, he has illuminated new fields of investigation and inquiry for all of us.

Maccoby sometimes minimizes the findings of recent
scholarship relating to the first century. Yet, that scholarship is indispensable as we move together to repair the
damage that has taken place in Christian-Jewish relations
during the ensuing centuries. I do not share Maccoby's view
that we must go back to a mythic explanation for Christian anti-Semitism. For me the answers are much closer to
the surface.

Strain as we might, with all of our linguistic, historical,
archeological, psychological, and spiritual resources—and
Hyam Maccoby has an abundance of these resources!—
there is so much about the life and times of Jesus that we
simply do not know, and that we may never know. Strain
as we might with the three Synoptic Gospels, and with
that most difficult of books, the fourth Gospel, the Book
of John (which plays such a key role in the Good Friday
liturgy), or strain as we might even with all of our modern
academic techniques and skills, we are still far from having
a full picture of that tumultous time when the Jewish people
were struggling under the yoke of brutal Roman occupation.

It was a time when, within two centuries, the Jews fought four bloody and unsuccessful wars of rebellion against the Romans, the last being a crushing defeat in the year 135.

Earlier there had been the destruction of the Holy Temple in 70, and the suicidal stand at Massada. It was a time of ferment when the Pharisees (how terrible a fate that creative religious group has suffered in history), the Sadducees, and the Essenes, and a host of other groups were all part of the vital religious life of Israel; a time of chaos, corruption, brilliance, courage, depravity, misery, ecstasy, beauty, degradation, life and birth, sickness and death. . . a time not unlike all times in human history. It was in such a time that Jesus of Nazareth was born, lived, and was killed by the Romans.

I perceive the rise of Christian anti-Semitism, stemming not from the myth of the Sacred Executioner, but rather as the story of a family rivalry; an unfortunate and highly verifiable reality in all our lives. As we all know, family rivalries are usually among the most intense and the most bitter.

Although Maccoby stresses that the early Christians were Jews, the point needs to be constantly reiterated since it helps explain the sense of rivalry that Christianity has historically felt toward Jews and Judaism. The earliest followers of Jesus were Jews, the first fifteen Bishops of the Jerusalem Church were Jews, the audiences who heard the preaching of Jesus were by and large Jews. Yet the canard that Jews somehow "rejected" Jesus has persisted; the Jews, it has been charged, "should have known better."

The anti-Jewish writings of the early Church fathers, especially those of John Chrysostom, have been rightly singled out for condemnation. His attacks on Jews and Judaism are vile and vulgar. Yet, as Robert Wilken has shown in his recent book, *John Chrysostom and the Jews: Rhetoric and Reality in the Late Fourth Century* (Berkeley: University of California Press, 1983), the Christian preacher was concerned and upset that many of his fellow Christians were attracted to the lifestyle and rituals of Judaism. Wilken believes that Chrysostom's real intention, while being highly negative about Judaism, was not the repression of Judaism. Rather, Chrysostom wanted Christians to attend church rather than the synagogue. The latter, Wilken believes, was a threatening rival to Chrysostom's church.

In the ninth century, bishops complained that rabbis were being sought to bless the agricultural fields owned by Christians. The rabbinic prayers were believed by Christians to be effective in producing good crops and harvests. But as Jeremy Cohen documents in his important work, *The Friars and the Jews: The Evolution of Medieval Anti-Judaism* (Ithaca: Cornell University Press, 1982), Judaism, by the thirteenth century was a religion of "error" in Christian eyes, and the belief that "error has no rights" had by that time become paramount. With that belief came increased anti-Jewish rhetoric and hostile actions, including the burning of the Talmud folios in Paris.

Earlier Christian leaders, including Augustine had affirmed the right of Jews to live as Jews, albeit in a Christian society. But by the Middle Ages, the notion of "one nation, one faith" had become widespread; these ominous words were to take on murderous implications that finally culminated in the cry, "one folk, one Führer, one nation" in our own century.

The task before us today is an awesome one. Simply put, the question before us is this: can Christianity commemorate the life and death of Jesus without placing blame upon the Jewish people of whom Jesus was a member? Can the authenticity of Christianity be maintained, even advanced, without the defamation of the people of Jesus? Can the Christian assaults against Jews and Judaism be ended, once and for all?

Maccoby believes this crucial task can only be achieved by radical surgery: a major redefinition of the divinity of Jesus, a reordering of the meaning of atonement, and a shattering, and an abandonment of the Sacred Executioner myth. I am not convinced of Maccoby's basic premise, nor am I confident that his prescriptions will be carried out by the Christian community.

My own recommendations are more modest, but I believe are more capable of realization than Maccoby's. Rivalries are usually ended when rivals are brought together, and are made secure in their own identities. Rivalries end when the root cause of such struggles is removed. In this case, it is the sometimes fanatical need of Christianity to lay, even force, its perceived religious truths upon everyone who does not share them. Special venom has historically been aimed at the Jews, the people who supplied the spiritual milieu for Jesus and the rise of Christianity.

When Christian sermons, hymns, liturgies, doctrines, teaching materials, indeed, when all aspects of church life are purged of the infantile rivalry disease, when the child can affirm with love the continued life and sacred existence of its parent, or if one sees the rivalry in sibling terms, when Christianity abandons its crushing attacks upon its older sibling, Judaism, and celebrates the joyous and mysterious reality of God being alive in both communities; only then will Christian anti-Semitism abate, and hopefully cease.

The restudy, the reinterpretation, the recasting, and ultimately the redefining of Christianity is one of the great tasks before us. It is to remove all vestiges of anti-Judaism while remaining true to the life-affirming message of Christianity. Time does not permit me to suggest in detail the specifics of such a change, but the outline has been sketched here today.

Can it be done? I am convinced that it can, but it will take a purposeful Christian community to undertake the absolutely necessary task of reversing nearly 2,000 years of the "teaching of contempt" that has so characterized Christianity's bitter rivalry with Judaism.

How painful that rivalry has been! The cries and whispers of my people still haunt us and drive us forward in our work. How painful it must have been, and is, for Christians, who are trapped in a theology of rivalry that has to defame and sometimes physically attack another people to legitimize their own existence. As God's children, both communities deserve better.

I do not share Maccoby's somewhat gloomy view of the various Christian statements, guidelines, resolutions, and pronouncements that condemn and repudiate anti-Semitism. He regards them as being of limited value. But just as anti-Semitism was transmitted to believing Christians through a series of earlier negative teachings and manifestos, so too, positive and authoritative teachings can be effectively employed in the war against Christian anti-Semitism.

Our generation has a rare opportunity to be remembered in future history as the generation that finally brought Christian anti-Semitism to an end. Using scholarship. albeit incomplete, using the powerful and compelling mandates of the Second Vatican Council and various Protestant resolutions and statements as driving forces for positive change, sustained by the magnificent achievements of religious pluralism in this country, and above all, driven by a fierce commitment to truth and to rectifying the bloody persecutions of the past, we should leave here today strengthened and enriched. Although Professor Maccoby has not finished the task for us, he has, with his probing mind and his searching spirit, goaded us to do more, much more. Can we do anything less than accept his challenge?

A Response to Professor Maccoby's Thesis

Rabbi Marc Tanenbaum

I am pleased to be here because I believe that Professor Hyam Maccoby's provocative thesis represents the beginning of an exceedingly important debate. Let me locate myself by saying that I find myself, both in terms of examination of history—religious, cultural and ideological history—as well as theological issues, somewhere squarely in the middle between Dr. Maccoby and Dr. Eugene Fisher. And that's not because I have a need to plant both of my feet squarely in the middle of the air, but rather because I think the dialectic which began here today is of real consequence.

This dialectic involves an examination of the whole question of the relationship of certain traditions in Christian teaching to Jews and Judaism, as well as an examination of more recent developments of profound importance, especially since Vatican Council II.

I think Dr. Fisher rightly said that these developments have not been adequately taken into account by Dr. Maccoby. Having said that, let me state at the outset what I appreciate in what Dr. Maccoby has done in this study. In this work, *The Sacred Executioner*, and in his earlier books he has raised up central issues to the level of public consciousness. In *The Judean Revolution*, among others, he has faced the centrality of the question of demonology which must be confronted more adequately, more profoundly than, I believe, most Jews and Christians engaged in the Jewish-Christian dialogue have been prepared to deal with thus far. And I am not sure that we have adequately dealt with these conceptions because we are far more creatures of the twentieth century enlightenment and its preoccupation with rationalism, social science and other categories. This rationalist mindset is inadequate to deal with the power of fanaticism, the power of demonology, the power of diabolizing, of dehumanizing which has dominated the greater part of the past 1900 years.

Now I want to address that demonological tradition and its power which continues to this day. And, in fact, I want to suggest that unless we find some way of recognizing the power of that diabolic appeal to human consciousness, its capacity to elicit fanatic responses which lead to the de-humanization of the other, and its capacity for creating a justification for destroying the other, we will not make progress on the deepest levels in relationships between Jews and Christians. Unless we are able to define the sources of that fanatic demonological world-view, we will simply not develop the categories and the basic conceptions which are essential for a method and technique for dealing with what is today the central threat in international law and order.

The Shi'ite Moslems—as a dramatic example—are operating on such a demonology and find all kinds of justification for destroying the other. Thus, Shi'ite Islamic theology assures that one may enter Heaven by being prepared to commit suicide in destroying "the enemy," "the Great Satan."

Dr. Fisher's statement, I think, is an important corrective in terms of articulating the ambivalences and ambiguities of Christian theological tradition regarding Jews and Judaism, and does require a far greater resonance in Dr. Maccoby's presentation of his thesis.

I had occasion to write a paper after Vatican Council II which appeared in a large volume issued by the University of Notre Dame, which shortly will be reissued. As I review the materials on the emergence of the Christian ambivalence of love-and-hate to Jews and Judaism, I was struck by the power of those affirmations which exist in Christian tradition even down into the Middle Ages which most Jews have simply screened out of their consciousness. That is probably due to the fact that the history of Jews and Christians has been for the greater part of the past 2,000 years so overwhelmingly an experience of oppression and denial. There is not enough moral energy left even to want to hold out the possibility that there were some important Christian affirmations about Jews and Judaism.

I believe that the Nazi Holocaust and all that has meant for the Christian conscience, as well as the tremendous needs of a new world of the twentieth century in which Christians and Jews together find themselves increasingly a minority in relation to a non-white, non-Judeo-Christian world, are compelling us to confront the deep realities of the relationship between Christians and Jews. Fundamentally, Christianity had never made up its mind as to where it stands in terms of its common patrimony with Judaism and its daily attitudes and relationships and behavior toward Jews. We find as we look into the history of the Christian-Jewish encounter for the greater part of the past two millenia that there have been teachings and episodes betokening the greatest of mutual respect and esteem between Christians and Jews. Thus, we find St. Athanasius, one of the early Church Fathers at the beginning of the fourth century, who said that "the Jews are the great school of the knowledge of God and the spiritual life of all mankind." St. Jerome, who lived in the fifth century and who spent forty years in Palestine where in Caesarea with Jewish scholars and biblical authorities he studied the Holy Scriptures and the Masoretic traditions—and from whom he obtained insights on which he based his translation of the Scriptures into the Vulgate—declared that "the Jews were divinely preserved for a purpose worthy of God."

This side of the affirmative attitude of the Church toward the Jews reflected the tradition of St. Paul in *Romans* 9 to 11, which speaks of Christians being engrafted onto the olive tree of Israel (11:17) planted by God. This tradition also found expression in positive behavior of popes even in the Middle Ages. Thus Callixtus II issued a bull in 1120 beginning with the words "Sicut Judaeis" in which he strongly condemned the forced baptism of Jews, acts of violence against their lives and property, and the desecration of synagogues and Jewish cemeteries. Gregory IX issued the bull "Etsi Judeorum" in 1233 in which he demanded that the Jews in Christian countries should be treated with the same humanity as with which Christians desire to be treated in heathen lands.

Side by side with that tradition there existed a tradition of hostility and contempt which the late French historian, Professor Jules Isaac, has written about in his various studies.[1] This tradition was perhaps most explicitly embodied in the eight sermons of St. John Chrysostom, who in the year 387 spoke from the pulpits of the city of Antioch to the first congregations of early Gentiles who became Christians, saying:

> I know that a certain number of the faithful have for the Jews a certain respect and hold their ceremonies in reverence. This provokes me to eradicate completely such a disastrous opinion. I have already brought forward that the synagogue is worth no more than the theatre. . . it is a place of prostitution. It is a den of thieves and a hiding place of wild animals. . . not simply of animals but of impure beasts. . . God has abandoned them. What hope of salvation have they left?
> They say that they too worship God but this is not so. None of the Jews, not one of them is a worshipper of God. . . . Since they have disowned the Father, crucified the Son and rejected the Spirit's help, who would dare to assert that the synagogue is not a home of demons! God is not worshipped there. It is simply a house of idolatry. . . . The Jews live for their bellies, they crave for the goods of this world. In shamelessness and greed they surpass even pigs and goats. . . . The Jews are possessed by demons, they are handed over to impure spirits. . . . Instead of greeting them and addressing them as much as a word, you should turn away from them as from a pest and a plague of the human race.[2]

Now, if one enters into the historic background and the context within which St. John Chrysostom made these remarks, perhaps one can understand a little better—one can explain but certainly not excuse—what led St. John Chrysostom to make these anti-Jewish polemics. It may be useful to take a moment to observe that the Church in the first four centuries of this era was struggling for its existence as an autonomous, independent faith community. In the minds of the Roman Empire the early Christians represented another Jewish sect. Judaism was the *religio licta* (a favored religion), and for early Christians to achieve any status, including the right to conduct Christian ceremonials, they had to come as Jews to achieve recognition by the Romans.[3] And so the early Church fathers found it necessary to separate Christians from the Jews. The early Christians felt very close to Jews; observed their Sabbath on the Jewish Sabbath, their Easter on the Jewish Passover. At the time of the Council of Elvira (ca. 300) many Christians in Spain thought the Jews had a special charisma as the People of God and therefore invited them to bless their fields so that they would be fruitful. To separate Christians from their associations with Judaism, to create a sense of autonomy and independence for Christianity, apparently in the wisdom of the early Church fathers it became necessary to embark on a drastic effort to break the bonds between church and synagogue and to give Christians a consciousness of difference from the Jews. In the process of this disidentification, however, the pattern of anti-Jewish attitudes and of anti-Jewish behavior became so entrenched, that by the time the Church became the established religion of the Roman Empire, these attitudes were reflected increasingly in ecclesiastical legislation. These laws subsequently led to the establishment of ghettos, the forcing of Jews to wear yellow hats and badges, and in general, this legislation reduced Jews to the status of pariahs throughout the Roman Empire. As the Church became the major institution integrating the whole of medieval society, the perception of the Jew within medieval Christendom became the perception of the Jew within Western culture and civilization.

The magnitude, the weight, the burden of that demonological conception of the Jews begins with Judas and becomes incorporated in the secular culture—and everything derives from that. As one faces the magnitude of that one realizes the need of the massive response to that demonology. And it will take more than minor modifications.

That is why the audience of Pope John Paul II in 1980, and again now,* is of such supreme importance. Only the power, the mystical power of the authority of the Holy Father of the Roman Catholic Church who has the capacity to say to more than 800,000,000 Roman Catholics throughout the world that the Church rejects this tradition. It is of another time, another culture, another history. We are in a new time and a new place. As the Pope declared in the statement to us, the new attitude in terms of the Catholic Church toward the Jewish people is one of respect, indeed, as he declares, of love which is profound and which the New Testament inherited from the Old Testament. The relationship today must be a break with the history of that past and a whole new series of responses are required to one another.

I must say to you the work of Dr. Eugene Fisher—which is based on earlier work with a dear friend and colleague with whom I was associated in Vatican Council II, Father Edward Flannery—has been monumental. Their profound commitment and dedication to facing every residue of anti-Jewish defamation, whatever its source, throughout the whole of the Roman Catholic Church in this country, in textbooks, in liturgy, in sermons, in providing adult education and audio-visual aids, are the hope of the future. We are enormously in their debt for their willingness, honesty, and candor as American Christians, who had nothing to do with the European experience, to face the full weight of those 2,000 years. They search for truth and justice to seek to bring about a new attitude, as the Vatican Council Declaration declared 20 years ago, of "mutual respect based on fraternal dialogue" and working together for the benefit of an ailing, broken and fragmented world by a common service to humanity.

---

*Ed. note: Rabbi Tanenbaum was a member of the American Jewish Committee delegation that had an extraordinary audience with Pope John Paul II on February 15, 1985.

NOTES

1. Jules Isaac, *Jesus and Israel*. Edited, and with a foreword, by Claire Huchet Bishop. Translated by Sally Gran. New York: Holt, Rinehart and Winston, 1971.

——————, *Has Anti-Semitism Roots in Christianity?* Translated from the French by Dorothy and James Parkes. New York: National Conference of Christians and Jews, 1961.

——————, *The Teaching of Contempt. Christian Roots of Anti-Semitism*. Translated by Helen Weaver. Biographical introduction by Claire Huchet Bishop. New York: Holt, Rinehart and Winston, 1964.

2. Martin Luther appropriated these anti-Jewish polemics and incorporated both the images and rhetoric in his "The Jews and Their Lies." See Eric W. Gritsch and Rabbi Marc H. Tanenbaum, *Luther and the Jews*. New York: The Lutheran Council in the U. S. A.

3. See James Parkes, *The Conflict of the Church and the Synagogue*. London: Soncino Press, 1934.

A Comment on Professor Maccoby's Thesis
Dr. Alan T. Davies

It is far too simple to reduce anti-Semitism to a single theory in this fashion: its roots are too varied, especially in the modern world. If Maccoby is correct, moreover, anti-Semitism would have been a kind of constant in Christian history and Christian piety which it has not been. On the one hand, it is scarcely a new idea to blame the deicide motif; deicide and the teaching of contempt associated with it are simply obvious factors, and tend to rise to the surface during stressful periods in Christian society. But the sacrificial view of the atonement is not the only view in Christian theology; in fact, it isn't even the classical view. Maccoby exaggerates the extent to which the notion of sacrifice is embedded in the core of Christian piety. On the other hand, Christianity has always contained other elements that tend to negate the anti-Judaic aspects of the tradition. Jews have not merely and certainly not consistently been regarded as mythic creatures of evil; they have also been admired (even during bad periods) and they have been the objects of sympathy (even in the Middle Ages). Neither Christian theology nor Christian policy has ever been consistent on the subject; moreover, Christianity itself exists in different forms, and some forms, for example Calvinism, have been less anti-Semitic than other forms. It is necessary to be far more contextual than Maccoby's rather monolithic explanation (which, by the way, Richard Rubenstein expressed in *After Auschwitz* long before Maccoby) suggests. There is no single Christian myth of redemption, and never has been. Consequently, what emerges is valid only as far as it goes, with respect to certain types of piety and popular theology during certain eras in societies in which the tendency to demonize alien and minority groups is strongly felt.

REPLY

Reply

Hyam Maccoby

Braham:

I thank the panel discussants for the formidable display of
erudition and critical analysis with which they have responded to the challenge of Professor Maccoby's thesis. I
warned him that such would be the case and now I am
confident that he is well-prepared to reply to the discussants' positions.

Maccoby:

Ladies and gentlemen, we have had a fascinating discussion;
and I'd like first of all to thank all the discussants for the
seriousness with which they've treated my views. Some have
agreed; some have disagreed. More have disagreed, but that
doesn't bother me. I find that I've got quite a lot on my
plate at the moment, and that's a situation that I relish. Let's
go through some of the comments that have been made
and see how they can be dealt with from the standpoint
that I put forward in my opening address. Now, first of all,
we had Dr. Fisher who had quite a severe criticism to put
forward about my views. He thought, if I may summarize
him rather baldly, that I was putting forward a view which
was a caricature. In fact, he even doubted whether I was
serious about it; but I assure him at this point I was. He
thought it was a caricature of Christian doctrine, and he
quoted various Popes and Councils in order to show that
the view that I was putting forward had no relation to
Christianity in its essence. He did say, however, and as a
matter of fact in this part of his speech he went even further than some of the other participants, that my analysis
was perfectly correct in relation to popular Christianity as

found, for example, in the Passion Plays. As far as popular Christianity is concerned, in fact, I got more wholehearted support from Dr. Fisher than I did from any other participant. But I'd just like to put to him the question: Is it plausible that there is this extraordinary gulf that he postulates between popular Christianity and official Christianity? It seems to me that if we have a religion which issues in a certain popular faith, we have an obligation not merely to say, "Oh, that's just what the people think; that's not real Christianity." We have an obligation to ask the question, "How did the people come to believe that? Was there anything in the religion that led them to believe that?" I am a great believer in the truth of the saying of Jesus: "By their fruits you shall know them." I think that was a very fine saying, and a very Jewish saying. In other words, if you want to assess a body of doctrine, don't put it on the laboratory table and dissect it; don't go to the pronouncements of theologians who have tried to work up the doctrine into a kind of philosophy. Go to the people and see how the thing is worked out. There's a famous saying in the Talmud which I could mention at this point to show this attitude of going to the people and seeing, if you want to know the truth. There was the great Hillel, the greatest rabbi of all. On one occasion he was faced with a great problem in *Halachah*, in the law, and he couldn't solve it. And he said to his disciples and to the other rabbis who were his colleagues, "I don't know how to solve this problem, but the people of Israel—they may not be prophets, but they are the children of prophets. Go and see what they do, and that may provide the answer." And they did; they went to see what the people did. And that supplied the answer, and Hillel accepted the practice of the people as the correct solution to that *halachic* problem. Of course, it's in a very different context from what we are talking about now; but, the general principle that I want to put forward is this: that the test, the practical test, of the doctrines of a religion is—how do they issue among the people? The people don't get it from nowhere. They get it from somewhere. It could be that the official doctrine might say one thing and the people do something else, and somehow or other the official doctrine seems to be powerless to affect the people. The people take a certain message even though the official expression of that message is different. How does that happen? I would suggest the way it happens is this: the most powerful thing in the world is a story. Theology is not powerful. I've been accused of being too cerebral in my approach. As a matter of fact I was accused of this by someone to whom in other respects I am most grateful for his most inspiring support, Dr. Everett. But he accused me of being too cerebral, and this was also put forward by Rabbi Rudin; that I'm putting forward a view which is somehow remote, based on all kinds of imaginations and scholarly theories and so on. I don't think that's true. I think what I'm saying is, look at the story; don't look at the theory, look at the story, because there's an old saying—don't trust the teller; trust the tale. And it's a story which is the basis of every doctrine whether religious or otherwise. I think that a group of people may become very powerful in history, but nothing makes them survive unless they've got a strong and powerful story. Look at the Mongols, for example. They made great conquests all over Europe and Asia. They disappeared out of history. Why? Because they had no story; they didn't have a story to orientate their life, to make them feel they knew where they were going, and therefore, they were easily conquered by another culture, the Islamic culture, which had a good story—a story all about a desert prophet, Mohammed who was raised by God. That's a story. Or take the Jewish story which is the story of a people saved out of a land of oppression, a people of slaves, liberated and brought to a "promised land." That's the basic story of Judaism. Now, it's useless telling me that this is not important compared with the creeds. If we look in the creeds of Judaism, we won't find much reference to that story. We'll find abstract principles. As a matter of fact, Judaism has never been a religion that cared much about creeds. I think Judaism has always recognized the fact that the story is paramount and the creeds secondary. For example, Maimonides under the influence of Greek logic tried to draw up a creed for Judaism. We find it in the liturgy, *The Thirteen Principles of Judaism*, but nobody ever agreed with him; it never became official, and the real essence of Judaism is not to be found in these creeds. The essence of Judaism is to be found in the story. And I think that if you're examining a religion, what you require is not that kind of analytical, theological approach at all; what you require is something like the approach of a literary critic who looks at a story and tries to assess what its characteristics are, what kind of effect it has, what view of life it expresses—because every story expresses a view of life. Now Dr. Fisher says the position of the Jews which I outlined, as the deicides, the people who performed the sacrifice, is not to be found in the creeds. I quite agree. The figure of Judas is not to be found in the creeds either. There's no Christian creed that even mentions Judas. That doesn't mean that Judas is a figure who is unimportant in assessing the kind of religion that Christianity is. I think the figure of Judas is a highly powerful figure, and this is not a cerebral approach to Christianity. It's an imaginative approach, and an approach which says, "Here is a story." What kind of story is it? And what is the story? It's a story of someone who goes to his death; he is not an ordinary human being. He is somehow descended from on high. He is a divine figure who has entered into a human body. This is a paradox, of course, how one can be human and divine at the same time. It seems to me that when Dr. Fisher said there's no such crime in Christianity as deicide, because Jesus was human as long as he was in his body, and therefore, it was only the body that was killed and not the God; this seems to me to be a somewhat legalistic "get out," because the essence of the story is that there is a person that is both a man and a god. I actually found that sort of "get out" in the opposite way when I once mentioned to some audience that I thought the doctrine of the death of Jesus was a case of human sacrifice. I was told, "No; it wasn't

human sacrifice because Jesus wasn't human; he was God."
So one can easily switch from one to the other. I mean, if
one is talking in a context where it's convenient to call him
human, he's human; and if one's talking in a context where
it's convenient to think of him as divine, he's divine. So I
think, there again we're not really taking the thing as a
story when we try to use bureaucratic categories of that
kind. We have a story and it's a paradox; there's a paradoxical situation of a man who is also a god. We also have
a paradox about the man who kills this man or about
Judas. Here's a paradoxical situation: somebody who is
wicked does a terribly wicked deed, and yet he's fated to
do that deed. How can he be wicked if he's fated to do it?
He's designated by Jesus; he's told, "I know you are the
one who's going to betray me." He even gives him the sop
to mark him out, "Go and do what you have to do." This
is a paradox. How can a person be fated to do something
and yet guilty for doing it? But again, that is the story element; this is what makes the story, that type of paradox.
And when I say that the position of the Jews is similar to
that of Judas I'm surely not making the position of the
Jews something very hard to grasp and cerebral. I'm saying
look at Judas Iscariot, a vivid character—fated to commit
a murder, and yet at the same time guilty of doing that
murder. If you try to take that character and explain it in
cerebral terms, in theological terms, you can go on forever.
I'm sure there are dozens of tomes of Catholic theology all
about Judas. That's not the point. The point is to grasp the
character in the story, and if you grasp the position of
Judas in that story, I'm saying you've already grasped the
position of the Jews in the Christian story, because Judas
is the individual who represents in that story the position
of the Jews in general. Now you may say, there's no Catholic theology which confirms that; there are no creeds
which confirm that. All that we've got is Passion Plays.
We've only got popular art, Passion Plays. We've got pic-
tures; we've got songs; we've got poems—that's only popu-
lism. *Only* popular. But what's more important than popular? After all, when you say "only the Passion Plays," the

gospels themselves are Passion Plays. The gospels are not works of theology; they all came later. Your theologians came later and tried to work it all up into a philosophy. The gospels are stories; they're Passion Plays. The writer J. M. Robertson said that long ago. And actually it [wasn't only] the gospels that were Passion Plays. There were Passion Plays enacted in relation to the god Adonis; there were Passion Plays enacted in relation to the god Attis. This idea of the death and resurrection of a sacrificed god giving rise to Passion Plays is quite common in the ancient world. So the genre of the gospels is that of a story. So that's all I'm saying: look at the thing as a story rather than as a theology and then you'll get further in understanding it and in countering the evil aspects of it. Now, just one more point about Dr. Fisher. He thought I was neglecting the fact that there are different epochs in Christian history, which is not all the same all the way through. This was a point that was read out in the name of Alan T. Davies as well at the end. Now, I'm not at all saying that anti-Semitism is exactly the same in all ages. I'm not even saying that the element of deicide or the element of being the Judas character is the only element in anti-Semitism. I made it clear that I thought it was only one out of three main elements. I do think it's the one that gives it the deepest bite, and therefore, it's the one that I emphasize. And I certainly don't think, for example, that Nazi anti-Semitism is exactly the same thing as Christian anti-Semitism. What I do say is that there would have been no Nazi anti-Semitism if it hadn't been for the previous Christian anti-Semitism. After all, all the Nazis were brought up as Christians; they stopped being Christian and they wished to continue hating the Jews. They could no longer give theological reasons for hating the Jews. They therefore, had to give other reasons for hating the Jews. I don't say they worked it all out in this kind of conscious way; but instead they brought up what they thought was a *scientific* reason for being a Jew-hater. It was no longer respectable to say they hated the Jews because they killed God. That was old-fashioned; they had to have a biological theory of race in order to rationalize the thing. This was something new. Actually, I rather disagree with Dr. Everett about race in Christianity. I think there *were* Christian racialists; but in general racialism has not characterized Christian anti-Semitism. Christians have always said, "If Jews become converted to Christianity, they will be accepted as Christians." Of course, it hasn't always worked out in practice, particularly in Spain. But in theory at any rate—and this time I do accept theory—there should be no such thing as racialism in Christianity, because a Jew who becomes converted to Christianity is a full Christian. So I do think that racial anti-Semitism is not the same thing as Christian anti-Semitism; but it never would have arisen without it. I think I've spent rather too long on Dr. Fisher, so I'll just mention that I do thank Dr. Everett for what I got from his very inspiring and very informative talk which brought out many, many points in relation to my own remarks. As a matter of fact he provided a very good answer, I thought, to Dr. Fisher on the point of popular anti-Semitism. He showed that popular anti-Semitism was far more important than Dr. Fisher *wished* to allow it to be. Rabbi Tanenbaum talked about demonology and he talked about the positive aspects of Christianity. Here, too, I want to say this (and I'll just finish with this point since we can't go on much longer): I do not wish to deny the positive aspects of Christianity. As a matter of fact, I believe more in the positive aspects of Christianity than many people who don't criticize Christianity as sharply as I do, because people come to me and say, "How can you criticize Christianity so sharply? There would be nothing left if they were to accept what you say." I say, "No; that's an insult to Christianity!" To say that Christianity would collapse because you take out of it those elements which give rise to anti-Semitism is an insult to Christianity. I think there's far more in Christianity than those elements which gave rise to anti-Semitism. There is a strand in Christianity which is much healthier than that sacrificial strain which has given

rise to anti-Semitism—for example, there are figures throughout the history of Christianity who have pointed to a different kind of Christianity. There is Pelagius, for example,
the great Pelagius, the antagonist of Augustine. I had an argument with a Jesuit leader in London, Father Corbishley,
and he said to me, "You don't have to argue with me—I'm
a Pelagian." And he was a Catholic theologian. Well, if he
was a Pelagian and if every Catholic said to me, "I am a
Pelagian," I would consider I'd won my point, because
Pelagius' type of Christianity was not a sacrificial type of
Christianity. There *is* an alternative tradition in Christianity. I believe it's there and I want to appeal to it. I'm not
trying to destroy Christianity at all; I'm trying to destroy
those aspects which are ruining Christianity.

ROUNDTABLE DISCUSSION

Braham:
Thank you Professor Maccoby. If the discussants have any counter-arguments I suggest that we spend the remainder of the time on a round-table discussion basis.

Dr. Fisher:
I would like to respond to this. I think Dr. Maccoby's response has very much helped to clarify certain points. His acknowledgment that it is possible within the creeds to articulate the essence of what Christianity is trying to say without that being anti-Semitic is really the core of my point. I had sensed you saying that Christianity is of necessity anti-Semitic. Such a position does not leave much room for further work or dialogue, so it is important when you allow for this possibility to articulate Christianity and the Christian story without anti-Semitism. I would not try to argue that that has always (or even often) been done perfectly in the church. But I believe there is more room here for dialogue than I had originally anticipated in reading your preliminary paper. An example would be when you're talking about the importance of Judas in the passion story. My example of that on a story level would be the creed where the story aspect of the creed works just as well with Pontius Pilate. The official creeds of the Church affirm that Jesus "suffered and died under Pontius Pilate." They do not mention any specific "Jewish" role in Jesus' death. Judas is not mentioned at all. What is important to Christian faith and is at its heart is the death and resurrection of Jesus and the confrontation with sin. Whether it's Pilate or not on the credo level is really irrelevant to that. It's very relevant on the historical level, and I'm not saying we can slough aside our grappling with history. But on the level of the story itself of what Christianity is trying to say

about the meaning of the death and resurrection of Jesus in terms of our perception of Jesus incarnate it is pertinent to the whole of humanity. My whole argument was really trying to say that it is possible to articulate that spiritual truth without trying to lay blame on any specific individual or group. The culprit of the story is sin—not "the Jews." I guess my essential reaction—You talk about the gulf between popular and official Christianity and use a moral critique rather than an intellectual critique, "by their fruits shall you know them." I think regarding that critique I would agree with you entirely. The fruits of Christianity and Christian-Jewish relations have not been something that I or I think any other Christian who knows enough about the history would care to defend. This implies that there has been over the ages something wrong with our teaching, which has not corrected our actions. My argument is that one can't simply say, "Aha! Here it is: The doctrine of the incarnation," and everything else is going to follow logically from that. If one looks at the doctrine of incarnation, a number of things could follow, so that that's where I think the difference lies. I would agree on the level of the moral critique. But I would insist on the doctrinal level that we have to take a more complex view than your scenario would allow. Because in fact, Christianity has spawned a number of different soteriologies on that and we can't just focus on one. Nor can the sacrificial element, which comes from the Hebrew Scriptures—God's revelation to us—be ignored or written off as "pagan."

Braham:
Thank you very much, Dr. Fisher. Dr. Everett, would you care to comment?

Dr. Everett:
I'd like to jump in on this popular versus classical or authoritative position. A couple of mentions have been made of Chrysostom's sermons against the Jews and how Bob Wilkens has shown that this is because people were more

interesting and the Jews led a life more appealing and so on. Really I think to try to say, therefore, we can't talk about Chrysostom as being perhaps the source of anti-Semitism; or if we have to talk about at least the ambivalence of the popular thing, I think is really asking a bit much of us, because in point of fact, when people study classical Christian theology, they don't study the fact that the populace at that time was sympathetic toward Judaism; they study the writings of Chrysostom and the writings of the church fathers in courses in seminary on the church fathers. And you do not get these glosses over these essays that say, "But you have to remember the reason they did this. . ." until recently. And maybe Wilkens is starting to— They weren't talking about the populace, and I think we have to ask why those in authority in the church kept struggling against this kind of popular sympathy toward the Jews, trying to keep their people from being more friendly with the Jews. And I think they have to ask themselves on what grounds were they attacking this friendliness with the Jewish community. I think they often went right to scripture to take lessons right out of John and Paul to try to be against that kind of friendliness. And I think that you can't as easily dismiss that—the linking of some of the church fathers to traditional anti-Semitic thought. I think you'll also have to ask where do the Passion Plays come from. These people did not sit around in little towns in Germany on some rainy October day saying, "Let's write a Passion Play," and make it up out of their heads. They went and got the basic story from the gospels themselves. And here I'm well rebuked on my criticism of the cerebralness of your message and the way that you talked about the story, because in point of fact, traditional theology has oftentimes come up with alternative theories to the "sacrificial blood atonement," those kinds of ideas of Christian theology. But I would wager that popular opinion in churches even today when you ask people what's the meaning of the death of Jesus and so on, is that He died for our sins because we were all sinful and God needed a way to

find a way to forgive us because we had, you, gone beyond
the pale—whatever you want to say there. And in that
sense, yes, the Jews do function in sort of an executioner
point of view. Why else resist the historical evidence that
says that they did not execute Jesus except that there's a
story floating around there that has a great deal of power
that we've been very resistant to give up; and the roots of
that story may be in the rivalry idea, though, that in order
to negate your main rival you paint him in such an immoral
position that there's nothing redeeming about them. I think
there's a lot of confusion of what's being talked about.

Rabbi Rudin:
You're playing for the very highest stakes in this rivalry.
You're playing for salvation, eternal light, what's your purpose here on earth and in life everlasting. Therefore, the
stakes are the highest. Second of all, Chrysostom is one of
the biggest, most vicious, vulgar, anti-Jew haters in the
world, but the very fact that Christian teaching has denied
even that little part that Wilken is bringing in, that he said
all those terrible things and he meant them, and he meant
more. But I'm not terribly interested in Chrysostom. He's
awful. But what was underneath that was that a rivalry
was going on—people were going into synagogues, people
were taking this seriously, people were listening to Jewish
sermons, and if you're going to have a rivalry and you've
got to displace somebody—you've got to destroy your sibling or your parent—then you just can't have that; then
you bring out the heaviest artillery that you can, and we
heard some of that today. And that's what Chrysostom
did and that's what all the others did. But remember if
rivalry is a myth and maybe Maccoby will think it isn't one
more mythical—I don't think it's a myth. I think rivalry is
very human and very real. Then you use all your artillery,
rockets, missiles, rhetoric to destroy the other one and to
kill the other people, because you have to for your own
rivalry reasons displace or replace. So no way I don't think
Wilken whom I don't know, but certainly no one was

defending or apologizing for Chrysostom. The tragedy is that Christian seminarians never got beyond the vicious, anti-Jewish rhetoric of Chrysostom and saw what was going on underneath.

Dr. Everett:
Well, I think you have to look at the church fathers as being a source of authority in terms of when people say, "How do we deal with Jews?" Let's go to Augustine; let's go to the gospels.

Rabbi Rudin:
And they offer this hideous description.

Dr. Everett:
And so when you have theologians telling their people, "Look, the deicide charge is wrong," and the people are coming back at you saying, "But we can prove it on the basis of the scriptures; who are you to tell us that the scripture isn't authoritative." I think that you really have an authority problem here that can't be dismissed even by simply looking at the sociological factors.

Rabbi Rudin:
Then you have to establish new sources of Christian authority.

Dr. Everett:
Absolutely. Or read them as the women do, with new eyes. I mean, the Feminist Movement which I have some problems with on other grounds.

Dr. Fisher:
You keep talking about that. . . .

Dr. Everett:
Has at least shown that the Christian community is open to the idea of re-evaluating their authority text and the way that they interpret classical Christianity.

Professor Maccoby:

Well, a couple of points arising out of this very interesting discussion here. First of all, on the question of authority which was raised by Dr. Everett, it seems to me that a saint is an authority; and if someone is canonized and if it is really thought in the church that anti-Semitism is an awful, dreadful sin, why is it never asked in relation to the canonization of someone whether he's an anti-Semite or not? Of course, this isn't such an easy question really. Recently I read about Father Kolbe—there's some talk about canonizing him—and it was suggested by people that he was an anti-Semite. Upon this, it was indignantly denied, "He is not an anti-Semite; he believes that the Jews had committed all the blood libels—every story he believes, but he forgave them all; and so he's not an anti-Semite." So it's not easy to establish in Christian terms what it means to be an anti-Semite. I would call Father Kolbe an anti-Semite; and the fact that he forgives us for committing things we never did I'd regard as adding insult to injury. But that's my definition of an anti-Semite. Perhaps it's not easy to explain to a Christian that Father Kolbe is an anti-Semite. And it does seem to me that when you get a few frigid pronouncements by popes condemning anti-Semitism, pronouncements which are never followed up in any systematic way in order to try to uproot this curse among the people; when on the contrary you get all the lower clergy reinforcing the anti-Semitic image, it does seem to me that the distinction between *popular* anti-Semitism and *official* anti-Semitism breaks down.

Dr. Fisher:

I've got to respond to this, because I think what I thought was a point of amity is now pretty much broken down. [Laughter] I mean, talking about a statement of the church such as *Nostra Aetate* as a "frigid pronouncement not followed up" is really a canard. . . .

Professor Maccoby:

I'm talking about earlier times. I said there's a new spirit now, but this is something that happened last Wednesday. And you can't talk about the whole Christian church in the light of something that happened last Wednesday. There's a new spirit now, I quite agree. But there is a tendency among Christians like yourself whom I honor for your approach to Jewish-Christian relationship, there's a tendency of wish fulfillment to say this is something that's always been happening throughout the history of the Christian church. It isn't; it's a very recent thing.

Dr. Fisher:

I didn't say it always had happened. My distinction was on different ground. And I also think that what one really needs is to look at those statements of the church and what has happened since then in much more depth. They have been followed up on—it's only beginning, granted; but certainly there's a lot more muscle to those statements than you would give them credit for. The presentation of Jews and Judaism in Catholic textbooks has improved drastically since the Second Vatican Council. That's a fact, not wish-fulfillment. And I think that is of critical importance to your theory, because again, with your theory that would be impossible. The other thing I want to mention is in terms of St. Maximilian Kolbe, who has already been canonized. An investigation of his attitude toward Jews was part of the procedure. He made, I believe, four brief and troublesome statements in his approximately seven hundred and eighty-five works. These do not refer to blood libel—but he did refer to Jews and Masons and the threat to society. It's much more complex than simply saying he was anti-Semitic. Yes, in one sense he was anti-Semitic; yes, he did accept—Somebody gave him an anti-Semitic and anti-Masonic tract that he reflects in those four statements. He did not spend much time on those; those were all glancing references. But that was looked at, and they felt that a person who sheltered Jews in his monastery, vigorously

opposed Nazism, and died in Auschwitz was the moral level
that they were trying to raise up: his death at Auschwitz,
his martyrdom for opposing Nazism with his very life. In
Catholic tradition you also have to remember that how
one dies says a lot about their life. They were looking at
what they thought was a martyrdom, which does wash
away previous sins. But they did look at that question and
that did hang up the proceedings for some months while
they investigated it.

Dr. Everett:
I think Dr. Maccoby has some grounds for attack here, because there were Polish partisans who were killed by the
Nazis and their mere death is a form of martyrdom, not
unlike the Father's, who were also anti-Semitic. And yet
we condemn them for their anti-Semitic activities in not
helping the Jews in Warsaw. And I don't see how we can
skirt the fence here on either Kolbe or the Protestants
who while opponents of the Nazis really were not clearly
opponents of anti-Semitism.

Dr. Fisher:
Kolbe clearly was an opponent of Nazism and that's why
he was picked up by the Nazis. And one of the things he
did in that period was open up his monastery to Jewish
refugees. Now one can argue that; I may not have the full
story. It's worth debating. But that's what they said. They
felt his saving deeds overcame his unfortunate words.
Again, that decision can be debated. But the integrity of
the decision should be respected, and certainly understood before it is denounced.

Braham:
At this juncture let me state that I don't think that we
could or did solve these problems that have plagued Jewish-
Christian relations for the past two thousand years. But I am
convinced that this conference has made great progress
in clarifying many of the issues underlying these problems,

and that we have made great strides in tackling the scourge of anti-Semitism. For this, and I know that I speak for everyone associated with the Institute and the Graduate Center, I am very grateful to the panelists—above all to Professor Maccoby for coming from London—and the other distinguished participants: the Reverend Everett, Dr. Fisher and Rabbi Rudin. Thank you very much for participating.

CONTRIBUTORS

REV. DR. ROBERT A. EVERETT is Pastor of the Emanuel United Church of Christ in Irvington, N. J. He received his doctorate from Columbia University in 1983 and served as Adjunct Professor of Religion at Albright College (1982-83) and at Lehigh University (1985). His academic interests include the history of Christian thought, the history of Jewish thought, ethics, anti-Semitism, and the Holocaust, and he is a recognized authority on James Parkes, the historian and theologian of Christian-Jewish relations. Rev. Everett's essays appeared in a variety of professional journals, including the *Journal of Ecumenical Studies; Christian-Jewish Relations; Christian Attitudes on Jews and Judaism;* and *Jewish Social Studies.* His essay "A Christian Apology for Israel" was included as a chapter in *End of an Exile* edited by Roberta Kalchofsky (Marblehead, Mass.: Micah Press, 1982).

DR. EUGENE J. FISHER is Executive Secretary of the Secretariat for Catholic-Jewish Relations of the National Conference of Catholic Bishops—the first layperson to hold this position. Appointed Consultor to the Vatican Commission for Religious Relations with the Jews in April 1981, Dr. Fisher is also active in several learned and professional societies, including the Catholic Biblical Association, the National Association of Professors of Hebrew, and the National Conference of Christians and Jews. He is the author of numerous monographs, including *Faith Without Prejudice: Rebuilding Christian Attitudes Toward Judaism* (Paulist Press, 1977); *Homework for Christians Preparing for Christian-Jewish Dialogue* (National Conference of Christians and Jews, 1982); and *Seminary Education and Catholic-Jewish Relations* (National Catholic Education

Association, 1983). Dr. Fisher has also contributed chapters to a large number of specialized studies and published a series of essays in such professional journals as *The Tablet: Journal of Ecumenical Studies; Christian-Jewish Relations; Midstream*; and *Judaism.*

HYAM MACCOBY is a fellow of the Leo Baeck College of London, where he teaches Talmud, Aramaic, and Apocrypha. He is the author of several highly acclaimed monographs, including *Revolution in Judaea* (New York: Taplinger, 1980); *Judaism on Trial: Jewish-Christian Disputations in the Middle Ages* (New York: Oxford University Press, 1982); and *The Sacred Executioner* (New York: Thames & Hudson, 1983). The latter, a study of the origins of anti-Semitism, aroused fierce controversy on both sides of the Atlantic. He is currently working on a book titled *The Mythmaker* to be published by Harper & Row (1986) and on a volume titled *Early Rabbinic Writings* to be published in the *Jewish and Christian Literature, 200 BC to AD 200* series by the Cambridge University Press. Professor Maccoby is a frequent contributor of articles and reviews to *Commentary; Midstream; The Times Literary Supplement; Encounter; The Listener; New Testament Studies* and other leading journals. He also contributed a chapter on the Bible to *The Jewish World*, edited by Elie Kedourie.

RABBI A. JAMES RUDIN is National Director of Interreligious Affairs of the American Jewish Committee. Prior to joining the Committee's national staff in 1968, Rabbi Rudin served as the spiritual leader of Sinai Temple in Champaign, Illinois (1964-68), and as Assistant Rabbi of Congregation B'nai Jehudah in Kansas City, Missouri (1962-64). A prolific writer, Rabbi Rudin's articles appeared in *Christian Century; Christianity Today; The Jewish Digest; The Jewish Frontier; The Jewish Spectator; Judaism; Journal of Ecumenical Studies; Midstream; The New Republic; Present Tense; Reform Judaism; Worldview* and other journals. He is also the author of several monographs, including *Israel for Christians: Understanding Modern Israel* (Fortress Press, 1983), *Evangelicals and Jews in an Age of Pluralism* (Baker Book House, 1983), and *Prison or Paradise? The New Religious Cults* (with Marcia Rudin; Fortress Press, 1980). Rabbi Rudin has lectured in all parts of the United States, and has been a frequent guest on many radio and television programs.

DR. MARC H. TANENBAUM, Director of International Relations of the American Jewish Committee, has a long and distinguished career in international human rights, world refugee, world hunger, and foreign relations concerns. In a recent national poll, Rabbi Tanenbaum was identified as "one of the ten most influential and respected religious leaders in America." He is a founder and leading member of the joint liaison committee of the Vatican Secretariat on Catholic-Jewish Relations and the International Jewish Committee for Interreligious Consultations, and of a similar body with the World Council of Churches. He was the only rabbi at Vatican Council II, and participated in the first official audience of World Jewish leaders with Pope John Paul II in Vatican City. Dr. Tanenbaum lectured at major universities, seminaries, religious and educational bodies in the United States, Europe and Israel, and at numerous national and international conferences. A prolific writer, he is the author or editor of several monographs and of a large number of articles.

DATE DUE

NOV 27 1990			